THE *KINGDOM*
in 1st Century
Christianity

THE *KINGDOM*
in 1st Century Christianity

Terry Stueck

High Plains Bible Mission Publishing
Albuquerque -- Atlanta

ISBN: 978-0-9961376-7-6 - Paperback
eISBN: 978-0-9961376-8-3 - eBook

⊗This paper meets the requirements of ANSI/NISO Z39.48-1992
(Permanence of Paper)

Unless otherwise noted, all Scriptures are taken from the *King James Version*.
Other Scripture versions are notated as follows:

BBE Basic Bible in English
CEV Contemporary English Version
DRA Douay-Rheims 1899 American Edition
ESV English Standard Version
GNB Good News Bible
GW God's Word
ISV International Standard Version
KJV King James Version
MKJV Modern King James Version
MSG Message Bible
NIV New International Version
TLB The Living Bible
VOICE The Voice
YLT Young's Literal Translation

120624

For seekers
who will not stop
until they discover
the height
the depth
and breadth
of what Jesus
said to find:
the Kingdom

———————

Matthew 6:33
Seek first the Kingdom of God
and be in good standing with its laws.

JESUS IS KING

CONTENTS

INTRODUCTION

Why were the early Christians fed to the lions? No other religious groups were fed to the lions. Jewish people were not fed to the lions. Neither were the folks who followed the ten major religions of Rome and the dozen minor religions. None of the visitors from far-away lands with strange religions were so persecuted. What was it about the Christians that turned them into enemies of the empire?

The answer lies in the vast difference between first-century Christianity and the religion that we have today. What you are about to discover will challenge your perspective as you discover original Christianity was a government and not a religion, a nation, not a church. It is no less than life-changing. It will alter the way that you live your Christian life and bring a clarity to the scriptures that, for many of us, has been lost for centuries.

In this book, we will dig deeply into the concept of kingdoms, the very foundation of the first-century believers' faith. Our current culture of anti-king and republic form of government erased long ago our knowledge of kingdoms and how they functioned. We have been bombarded by the frailties and faults of the worst of the monarchs. We have lost sight of five thousand years of historical kings and kingdoms, the majority of which flourished and were successful. We have also lost our way in scriptural inquiry into God's plans for kingdoms and why He Himself instituted the kingdom as His form of government. It is so important to Him that He calls Himself "the King of Kings."

My journey to the Kingdom, where I am now a law-abiding citizen, took a major leap forward around the turn of the century, when I made an incredible spiritual voyage toward a forgiving lifestyle. As a result of that trek, I wrote a book so others could follow, titled *Forgive Instantly & Live Free*. The first half of the book lays out the two parts of forgiving that it takes to free both parties: the offender and the offended. The second half gives the secret to instant forgiveness, which is the ownership of God. He owns all things, including me. Discovering the depth of God's power in His ownership is what transformed my future.

That question of ownership led me to write another book, *Being God: Stealing God's Power, Glory, and Kingdom*. The task of writing that treatise took me into the depths of a fundamental truth that we in America, and now around the world, are averse to. The book is a full expansion of the New Testament principle "you have been bought with a price," as put forth in 1 Corinthians 6:20.

We like to own things, including our own lives. I once had the opportunity to present the Gospel to a vice admiral (three stars) of the US Navy. As I laid out the price that Jesus had paid for us, he immediately responded: "I don't want to be owned by God." Never before in my life of witnessing had a party so adequately understood the door of salvation and known clearly the reason why he rejected it. He expressed the motive of many in the human race who don't know how to put their refusal into words. We have songs like "My Life" by Billy Joel and "My Way" by Frank Sinatra. "Mine" is one of the first words that we learn on our own as children; no one teaches it to us.

That book landed me in the domain of the Kingdom. I did not know about the Kingdom at that time, but I was basking in the newfound freedom of letting God own and take over every aspect of my life. Suddenly, living had become easy. I knew I was in the promised land, "the rest" as put forth in the book of Hebrews.

Hebrews 4:9 (KJV)
There remaineth therefore
a rest to the people of God.

I discovered "the Kingdom" after a decade of pursuing Jesus and intensely studying the Gospels and the book of Acts, which is where you find Him. I was committed to following Jesus as He had requested of me. "Follow me" were His exact words. That meant going to where He was portrayed and quoted. I wanted to know Him and step in His footprints. In my first reading of the scriptures as a new believer, it had intrigued me that the early believers were willing to give all that they had to the newly formed flock. Mistakenly, I had associated the events around the gift of Ananias and Sapphira in Acts chapter 5 with the statement in Acts 4 that they had all things in common, leading me to conclude they had given away everything they had to the common group. One particular gift, however, does not imply everything that they owned. It was a large gift, but not necessarily their entire net worth.

I went back to Acts 4:32 to explore what they meant by common ownership. It did not mean that they gave things away, but rather that they shared all that they had as though all in the group were owners of the assets. I checked the translation options to discover the word "commonwealth." I had heard that term associated with four of our states: Kentucky, Massachusetts, Virgina, and Pennsylvania. Since those states are commonwealths in name only and not in practice, little can be learned from them concerning the day-to-day functioning of a commonwealth. I checked the dictionary to dive more deeply into that translation. To my surprise, there was the word "kingdom." It was enlightening to discover that kingdoms are commonwealths. In a kingdom, the king owns everything, but he shares ownership with his subjects willingly.

Bingo! Hold your cards. Can there be a mistake? The light just came on. Right there it was; they were functioning as a real, vital, living kingdom. They were not a religious group, but a new nation of subjects of the newfound king, Jesus. They considered their possessions to be the property of the kingdom and, therefore, the wealth was held in common for all to use and share. Everything in scripture came together in that truth. I had found the hidden kingdom. With a fresh new anointing of that revelation, I began the most exciting study of my Christian life diving into the reality of the Kingdom. I already had been resting in the King's domain, and now I had sight of the King. The word "kingdom" is a contraction of two words: king and domain. I had made the discovery that all of humanity is searching for, one of God's greatest gifts to us—the Kingdom of God.

Luke 12:32
Fear not, little flock; for it is your
Father's good pleasure to give you the
kingdom.

You are about to journey into the most exciting adventure of your Christian life. In the following pages, I will lay out the Kingdom so simply that you can comprehend what the world cannot find. They are unable to grasp that Jesus is no longer in a manger, or on a cross, or seated teaching children dressed in ancient tunics. Rather, He is seated on His throne in Heaven as the King of Kings. They cannot see that the kingdom is here now, a borderless Kingdom in the hearts of true followers. They are missing the Kingdom that Jesus delivered at His first coming and are totally unaware of their deficiency.

Not only do we want to look afresh and anew at kingdoms, but we want to understand God's mind in His creation of them. We will look at the success of benevolent kings in scripture and in real-life examples today. You will see the Bible in a fresh, new perspective that will make you say, "How did I miss that?"

I learned that I was not the only one who found the Kingdom. Throughout history are Kingdom believers who knew and lived the Kingdom life. We will learn the Kingdom life is the Christian life that Jesus intended for us. The proof comes from His own lips. Get ready for the greatest journey of your life, following Jesus in His exact footsteps.

The Challenge: Read It for Yourself

The Roman Amalgamated Religion and its offspring have diminished the use of the Bible. They depend on liturgy and doctrine written by men rather than the words of Jesus. Even the Reformation emphasized Paul's writings over Jesus's words. They teach the books of the Gospel to be a fulfillment of the Old Testament and therefore less relevant than Paul's writings. The Kingdom has been intentionally hidden by those who would rather be king than serve the real King. Ever since the Garden of Eden, man has sought to elevate himself above the King of Kings. Ego keeps us from the Kingdom and hides it through the exaltation of man in religion. The serpent in the Garden of Eden tempted Adam and Eve by enticing them with the concept of being God or equal with God. Who was God? He was and is the King of Kings. We tend to follow their pattern. We still find it difficult to give God His rightful place at the top of the chain of command.

It must be stressed that Jesus is the source of our faith. Paul and all others are commentators, not the source. No statement by any human, even one under inspiration, can ever nullify or change what Jesus proclaimed. Theologians and denominations twist the words of Paul to meet their own requirements in support of doctrinal positions unique to each. Jesus's words will never pass away. In spite of men denying, minimizing, and marginalizing them, His words are still our source.

Matthew 24:35
Heaven and earth shall pass away,
but my words shall not pass away.

Before you toss this book aside, let us take a fresh look at what Jesus actually said and taught in the Gospels. Let's see again, with clear eyes, not shaded by past theological arguments, how the book of Acts actually portrays the new believers. We will look at what we may have missed. Most denominations have been so obsessed with particular themes that they have missed Jesus as King. In so doing, they are blind to His real purpose in reestablishing the Kingdom of God on earth as a vital, living nation.

I am not asking you to take my word for what Jesus or the scriptures say. We don't need another human opinion on Bible interpretation. We just need to see the scriptures through a clear lens not tainted by those who have already muddied our thinking. We will not challenge doctrines, but we will ignore them so that Jesus can tell the story instead of theology books written by men.

Let's see what we missed. Let's pull the scales from our eyes and see what is in plain sight. How many times have we read it and failed to perceive what was clearly written? May the Lord open our eyes. Understanding the Kingdom is easy, if only we can see past the prejudices that blind leaders who never found the Kingdom have taught us. Kingdom living is the life that God intended for Adam and Eve. He intends this life for us today as well.

Matthew 7:14
Because strait is the gate, and narrow is the
way,
which leadeth unto life, and few there be that
find it.

CHAPTER 1

Shadow Government

A Shadow Nation,
not Visible on a Map
A Kingdom, not a Theology
A Government, not a Religion
Citizens, not Members
Followers, not Lawyers
Servants, not Theologians

Acts 17:6–7 (VOICE)
These people—they're political agitators turning the world upside down! They've come
here to our fine city, and this man, Jason, has
given them sanctuary and made his house a
base for their operations.
We want to expose their real intent:
they are trying to overturn Caesar's sensible
decrees.
They're saying that Jesus is king, not Caesar!

Early believers functioned as a kingdom, a separate nation. While living physically in the Roman Empire, they had their allegiance to another government, that of the Kingdom of God. Their group was not a religion but a country, a separate nation, with a king as its government. It had its own laws and citizens. It was borderless in that it existed in the hearts of men wherever they were. The size of the nation was the largest of all kingdoms, because it extended to the corners of the world, wherever believers went.

Even though we speak in the past tense as we describe what the first three centuries of followers of Christ were like in their beliefs and practices, we must call attention to the fact that the living vibrant Kingdom exists today. Since Jesus reestablished the Kingdom of God, it has never ceased. It has been overshadowed by a replacement organization that was more a religion than a nation. There still exist quiet underground groups and individuals of Kingdom Christians. They are still marginalized and persecuted by the accepted orthodox culture of the day.

The Kingdom of God is the most radical idea that God ever brought to earth. It is a government ruled by God Himself as its king, the King of Kings. His throne is established in the heavens, where He rules earth as a colony. He established its laws with His spoken word. He chooses its citizens to populate it. He staffs the colony with under-kings and royal citizens, who are considered His children. They are also priests because of their direct access to God. Just as King George III ruled the American colonies from abroad in England, so God rules the earth from heaven afar.

When we say God is King, we are referring to the visible image of God, which is Jesus. We must understand the view that the early Christians had of the Trinity. It is much different than our present-day view, which is influenced by the imitation organization that draws on ten other religions to amalgamate an all-encompassing view that enmeshes them all. Most Christians currently define the Trinity as three distinct persons. That is because of the centuries of teaching influenced by the Roman trinity: Zeus, Aphrodite, and their son, Apollo. These Roman gods were distinct persons. Our God is not.

The early Christians' analogy of the Trinity was to view God as the sun and Jesus as the beams of light that come from the sun. That makes them inseparable. Jesus is just the visible part of God that we can see. To early Christians, Jesus and God were the same, one the visible part of the other. The Holy Spirit was the heat waves from the sun, while Jesus was the light waves. All three are the same manifestations of the sun. That is why, when John saw his vision of heaven, he saw only Jesus on the throne. Jesus is the visible manifestation of God. Because they are inseparable, not three distinct persons, but all of God is on the throne at the same time. We only see God on the throne as Jesus because He is the only visible image that our eyes can capture.

Colossians 1:15
(*Jesus*) Who is the image of the invisible God.

John 10:30
I and my Father are one.

Early Christians did *not* have an underground religion. They had a shadow government, and they did not hide it. They openly declared their allegiance to King Jesus. They were described, in Acts 17:7, as declaring Jesus to be their king rather than Ceasar. They were citizens of an unseen Kingdom that exists in the hearts of men, a Kingdom without borders.

Timeline

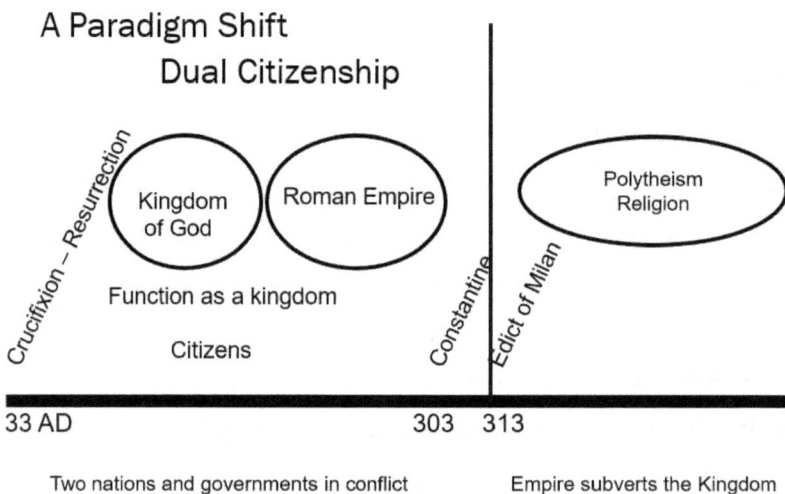

Emperor Constantine was faced with a dilemma. The Kingdom of God was out pacing the Roman Empire. To save the Empire, he, along with some provincial leaders, devised a plan to transform the structure of Christianity into something they could control.

Men have invented many religions. All of them place obligations on people and make them feel good for doing something to please God. Humans get satisfaction from religion. An individual makes a decision, prays a prayer, worships, gives, and participates in a host of activities that earn them credit as they perceive them to be valuable. Conversely, the Kingdom has but two things to do: get in the Kingdom, and stay in the Kingdom by being law-abiding. Then, as a law-abiding Kingdom citizen, one has all the rights and privileges that come with citizenship.

Acts 17:6 (ISV)
These fellows who have turned the
world upside down have come here, too.

It was the statement of an outsider, a nonbeliever, who declared the followers of Jesus were the people "who turned the world upside down." What was it that made them so different than what we see in the current version of Christianity? What did they have or know that we have somehow lost? Was it a higher level of dedication? What made them willing to share all their possessions for the good of the community? What drew them so tightly together that they had unity? What motivated them so much that they were willing to suffer death over disavowing their founder? How did they manage to do these things for nearly three hundred years?

Finding the answers to those questions becomes more difficult as we move further along in the human timeline. Isaiah 53:6 tells us, "We have turned everyone to their own way." If that is true, then we continue to drift farther from God and not closer. We like to have our own way. And the farther we drift, the harder it is to know the mind of God. We have killed and exiled the kings of this earth so that we can have it our way. Democracy is not the effort to find the will of God, but the demand of men to have their own way. It is the will of man perfected. We shall not have a king rule over us. Yet we continue to seek a leader who can solve all the problems and dilemmas. Religious folks believe Jesus will someday return, set up His Kingdom, and rule on earth for a thousand years. The truth is simpler. He already is King and has a Kingdom that extends to the earth colony. But someday, He will move his throne here and be present in the colony. Then every knee shall bow. Right now, only his citizens willingly bow.

Isaiah 45:23

I have sworn by myself, the word is gone out
of my mouth in righteousness *(justice)*, and

shall not return, that unto me every knee shall bow, every tongue shall swear [allegiance].

Romans 14:11
For it is written, As I live, saith the Lord, every knee shall bow to me, and every tongue shall confess to God.

Philippians 2:10
That at the name of Jesus every knee should bow, of things in heaven, and things in earth, and things under the earth.

How Could We Have Missed It?

The Kingdom of God is a monumental directional change in our way of living. We have elevated ourselves and our form of Christianity and feel we are right in our practices. We fight with each other over doctrine and are positive that we have the correct interpretation of God's word. We are so confident in our Christian structures that we exclude others who deviate even a little from what we hold to be Christianity.

One can easily see how other groups would be surprised to learn that they have been wrong and trekked off in the wrong direction for decades, if not centuries. But the shock comes when we too must admit we also have missed the message Jesus delivered and the goal that He wanted us to achieve.

Getting to the true core of Christianity implies understanding the very foundation of who Jesus is and what He came to do. He was born a king, with full bloodlines traced though His father and mother back to King David *(see appendix A)*. But more importantly, they can be traced to Adam, the only other person who could claim to be a direct son of God. We claim to be sons of God through a spiritual rebirth, but only Adam and Jesus could claim to be sons of God in their physical formation.

Luke 4:43

He said unto them, I must preach the kingdom of God to other cities also: *for therefore am I sent.*

Jesus did not come to start a religion. Jesus came to restart the kingdom that Adam had lost. Adam did not lose a religion; he lost a kingdom. The chain of command from the King of Kings down to Adam was surrendered, as Adam obeyed the evil one rather than God. The cross was only a step in the path that would lead to the restoration of the Kingdom. The good news of the salvation message is only part of Jesus's good news. He had a fantastic nation He invited you to join. We fall short when we fail to offer the Kingdom to new converts. The Kingdom was Jesus's goal, and the cross was the means to get there. The larger goal is to enter the Kingdom. Kingdoms have kings. Losing sight of Jesus as King leaves one without a kingdom.

Isaiah 9:6

For unto us a child is born, unto us a son is given: and the *government* shall be upon his shoulder:

Isaiah declared the government would rest solely upon Him. He did not say that the Messiah would have the church or a religion on his shoulders. We have allowed Christianity to become a religion when God's original purpose was to have a nation. Nearly all denominations recognize that Jesus will return to set up a kingdom. Kingdoms are nations with a form of government, not a form of religion.

Religion and government are two different animals. They don't mix. We even have some denominations who pride themselves on separation of church and state, more proof that government is in a different category. Let us dive into the Kingdom and leave behind the arguments of religion.

CHAPTER 2

Kingdoms Are Commonwealths

Acts 4:32
And the multitude of them that
believed were of one heart and of one soul:
neither said any of them of the things which
he possessed was his own; but they had *all
things common.*

The early followers of Jesus called themselves "the Way." Their critics and detractors called them Christians as a derogatory term, but believers followed Jesus's words as He called Himself, "the Way," the truth and life (John 14:6). "Way" fit the movement well because it was "a way of life" and not a religion. It was a movement centered on how to live the Christian way of life. It was a functioning kingdom, not a religious system of ceremonies. It was a nation in the hearts of men, with a king, a type of government just as it had been delivered to Adam. It was totally different than what we practice today in many circles of Christianity.

The early followers of the Way had found the great treasure, the pearl of great price. They had found the Kingdom and were willing to trade their lives and their possessions to have it. Jesus had accomplished what He had come to do, to restore what Adam had lost. God did not give a religion to Adam, He gave a dominion. The treasure, the valuable pearl of great price referenced in scripture, is the Kingdom once delivered to Adam and now restored through Jesus. Jesus brought the Kingdom with Him when He came here. He taught it and offered it to the Jews first, and then to the Gentiles.

Acts refers to the early converts as having all things in common. Strong's concordance lists "common" as the translation of the Greek *koy-nos'*, which means shared by all or several. That term, today, is condensed into just one word: commonwealth. A commonwealth is a political community founded for the common good. The noun "commonwealth," meaning "public welfare, general good or advantage," dates from the fifteenth century. The term literally means "common well-being."

E. Stanley Jones discovered the Kingdom while visiting Russia. Jones was a missionary to India in the early twentieth century. Russia had lost their king to the Bolshevik revolution in 1917. While visiting the country, he met many Russians who lamented the loss of their commonwealth kingdom and gave him insights to the successes of that form of government. He connected the dots to what he saw in the book of Acts and became a lifelong advocate of the Kingdom of God. Just before he died in 1972, he published his most famous work, *The Unshakable Kingdom and the Unchanging Person.*

In contrast to the magnificent concept of living under God's direct rule, mankind invents religious systems that he can lead without God. The Pharisees were one of those systems Jesus had to defeat. He called the Pharisees lawyers. Lawyers is a government word, not a religious term. Everything to Jesus was in government terms. They were the religious legal know-it-alls of their day. Our present world has its share of the same, but few of them have a clue as to what the real live Kingdom is about. They know doctrine and can quote verses, but the true Kingdom is not within their grasp. Just like the Pharisees, they have taken away the knowledge of the Kingdom and prevented their followers from finding it.

Matthew 23:13

But woe unto you, scribes and Pharisees, hypocrites! for ye shut up the kingdom of heaven against men: for ye neither go in yourselves, neither suffer them that are entering to go in.

There is a time when it is necessary and appropriate to reach out and give a hand up to those who desire to find the Kingdom. The Kingdom is the treasure that you are willing to sell everything so that you have enough to buy the field where the treasure lies buried. Jesus gave the illustration of the pearl of great price as a metaphor of the Kingdom. His mission was to restore the Kingdom back into our hands here on earth. The Kingdom is that pearl of great price, the treasure worth more than all the wealth of the world.

Some believe Jesus is the pearl of great price. Jesus is very important to the Kingdom message because He is the door to the Kingdom. When I buy a house, the door is very important. A house without a door is not usable, but I want more than just the door. I want the house behind the door also. I want the whole package. I not only want Jesus; I want the Kingdom. He opens the access to it. Jesus described Himself as the door but went on to encourage finding the good green pasture that lies beyond the entrance.

John 10:9
I am the door: by me if any man enter in,
he shall be saved, and shall go in and out, and
find pasture.

Many have been given a mental roadblock. We have been told the church is the Kingdom. But what if that is not true? What if the church is not the Kingdom? The church has no king, nor does it have a domain. It certainly has no dominion over you, even though it tries to gain that control.

Others believe and teach the Kingdom is far off in time waiting for Jesus to come and set up His realm. But what if that is not true? Who said He has to come to set up His Kingdom? Can He not set up His Kingdom from afar and oversee its functions from His present vantage point in heaven? Isn't He God? "Is anything too hard for the Lord," Genesis 18:14 proclaims. Besides, He already came to earth two thousand years ago and accomplished that task. Could it be that He set up His Kingdom then, and we have missed it because an evil force has hidden it? Has it been hidden because someone or something doesn't want us to find it? Could it be the devil, or is it men who want to rule in place of the real king? Either would be a likely answer. The most sobering thought is that we have hidden it from ourselves because of our innate, inborn desire to rule our own lives.

Most seminaries and Bible colleges do not teach anything about a present, real, functioning kingdom. Neither do you hear many correct messages on the Kingdom from the pulpits. We hear the Kingdom is not here yet, but will be someday. We hear the church is the Kingdom. Only a few current-day songs reference Jesus as King. Jesus is portrayed from the pulpits as a baby in a manger, a savior on the cross, in the tomb, risen, and ascended, but not as a king. Yet, the Gospels mention "king" and "kingdom" two hundred seventy-five times. Jesus declares His Gospel, His Good News, to be the Kingdom, not the cross. The cross was an agony to Him, while the message of His kingship was His thrust and joy. The message of the current-day Christian world is personal salvation by way of the cross, while the message of the early believers was a new citizenship in a fantastic kingdom by way of Jesus as your savior king. The Way had a much broader message. It presented Jesus as the door, but went on to give the proper way to live the Christian life as a citizen and servant to the King. To serve the king means to obey the king. There, again, is the law-abiding citizen concept.

In my quest for information about the Kingdom, I found pastors and churches who are on the right track. They preach and pursue the Kingdom. Churches can be kingdom-minded and help their members achieve Kingdom knowledge and citizenship. I found them to be few in number, but profound in their efforts. There is no reason a church cannot go on to explore and expound the living vibrant Kingdom that flourishes in the shadows of our current times.

Through these pages, I intend to help you dig up the pearl of great price. Some years ago, I found the pearl that Jesus indicated few would find. The devil does not want us to find the Kingdom. Many religious institutions do not want us to find something that would pull our attention and affection away from themselves. Far too often, a denomination and its growth have become more important than the King. But most of all, the Kingdom is hidden by our own ego that places ourselves high in our worldview. We are locked in our own self-exaltation and desire to be in control. We would have fought for the rights to own property privately and to vote if we had lived back in colonial revolutionary times. We like to own things, including ourselves. Giving up control to the King is not easy once we have tasted "our own way."

Isaiah 53:6
All we like sheep have gone astray;
we have *turned everyone to his own way;*
and the *Lord* hath laid on him the iniquity of
us all.

CHAPTER 3

The Upside-Down Kingdom

Proverbs 14:12
There is a way
which seemeth right unto a man,
but the end thereof are the ways of death.

Proverbs 21:2
Every way of a man is right in his own
eyes; but the *Lord* pondereth the hearts.

The Kingdom will turn our world upside down, just as Jesus did two thousand years ago. We need to grow past the religious regiments and try to receive and live in the great gift that God gave us, His Kingdom. We need help to find an entirely new way to relate to God as our King. We will first need to clean the slate and wash it of the chalk dust that covers it. We have been taught incorrectly and willingly received it because it was easy. Teachers found ways to ignore some verses and twist statements of the apostle Paul to build a religious case well short of God's ultimate goal.

The current-day Gospel only takes you halfway to the goal that He has for you. The only way we can reach the destiny intended for us to be delegate kings and deputy rulers is to first submit to the King of Kings. This name implies that there are kings under Him. What we have hunted for has been at our feet all along, but we were looking up instead of down. It is in the opposite direction from where we thought. Instead of fighting to get to be king of the hill, we need to follow the one who can make us the kings, as Adam was before the fall. You can be a king, but you can't be the King of Kings. That ultimate desire to be equal to or greater than God is what upended Adam in the Garden.

The culture tells us we have to climb, push, struggle, beat others to it, and be the toughest to win the top of the hill and be crowned king. The opposite is true. All we have to do is follow the real living King and gain His favor. He will set us as a king of our own domain under His authority. There is a real functioning Kingdom, alive and well, on the planet *now*. We can find it if we are willing to clean the slate of what we thought or learned. He must increase, we must decrease.

Everything Jesus taught is completely opposite to

man's thinking. Man believes revenge is acceptable, but Jesus said to love your enemies. Culture teaches an eye for an eye, but Jesus said turn the other cheek. Humanity wants to own things, but Jesus said, if someone asks for your coat, give them your shirt also. The world is wrought in self-promotion, but Jesus said love your neighbor as yourself. The human race has a hundred agendas to pursue, from money to fame, but Jesus said seek the Kingdom first. To follow Jesus is an about-face on every topic you have ever held dear. Staying in His footsteps will turn your world upside down.

A Lifelong Seeker

Many people vacation in cities and tourist areas when they have the opportunity. Others travel to state and national parks. I have this burning desire to seek out what lies beyond the end of the roads, where only a few wild animals call home. I have always gone long past the places that most folks call far enough.

I was raised far away from city life in the Iowa countryside. Our nearest neighbor was a mile away. A few cars passed our farm every day, but it was common to not see anyone for days or weeks during the summer when school was on break. As a young boy, I hunted and trekked across miles of forests, streams and wilderness areas, alone in search of the beauty, awe, and amazement of what I might find.

It was that seeking and searching that took me to far-away places that few have seen. Traveling to Alaska was not far enough for me. The road to Alaska in the '80s was a twisting, turning mess of gravel and mud. Oil had been discovered at the shores of the North Sea, so they scratched out a trail for trucks to get to the North Slopes on what they called the "haul road." It traversed the four hundred fifty miles from Fairbanks across the Brooks Range and the North Slope tundra all the way to Prudhoe Bay. The surface was large gravel rocks meant for the heavy loads carried by truck tires. That inner quest to seek the beyond took me across that expanse of North Alaska. There, I discovered a hundred thousand reindeer and a billion mosquitos. I also discovered that the way back was as hard as the way there.

Traveling four miles an hour up the Amazon River a couple hundred miles from Iquitos, Peru, was not far enough. I had to take the houseboat up the backwaters of the Napo River into the back side of Ecuador. Far across New Mexico, through the open desert from Acoma Pueblo to Pie Town on cow trails, through arroyos without a road or a person in sight for a hundred miles, that was my forte. Deep into the Andes on cliff-hanging roads, there you would find me seeking out unknown towns and villages with the gospel in hand.

It was that seeking, that never-give-up, never-quit attitude that led me to do the impossible one day some twenty years ago. I was determined to do what Jesus said, "Follow me." That was a quest that would lead to the farthest reaches of human endeavor. I set myself to concentrated study in the Gospels. If I was going to follow Him, I had to know and hear Him. For too long, I had followed denominations and church leaders. I had followed what others had written. Now, I would concentrate on Him. There are two words that exclude all others: "follow *me*." Not follow the scriptures, not follow Paul, not follow the New Testament, but "follow *me*."

That seeking, asking, and knocking opened my world to the King of Kings. In digging deeply into the original languages, seeking to know not just what He said, but what He really said in His language and what He meant, I discovered the pearl of great price. It was right there in plain sight. Only my blindness had kept me from finding it sooner. Once I saw it, it was everywhere. Once you see it, you can't unsee it. The kingdom that God gave Adam has been restored and given to us, if we will only seek it with our whole heart. If you are willing, if you are brave, if you are humble, if you fear not, if you are willing to pay the price, it's yours. Matthew 6:33 beckons us to seek first the Kingdom of God and be in right standing with its laws.

In our current culture of the Christian religion, our churches invite hearers to accept Jesus, or put their faith in Him for salvation. The invitation ought to include the invitation to accept Him as savior/king and be a citizen of the Kingdom. Churches usher the new convert into church membership, but usually not into Kingdom citizenship. Becoming aware of one's new citizenship would simplify Christian living and help strengthen new believer's biblical understanding. If unity comes to the Christian world, it will only be by way of the kingship of Jesus and an obedient relationship to Him as King. Having many leaders results in disunity. Uniting behind the single King of Kings would reproduce the unity they had in the first three centuries.

John 13:34–35
A new commandment I give unto you, that
ye love one another; as I have loved you, that
ye also love one another.
By this shall all men know that ye are my
disciples, if ye have love one to another.

CHAPTER 4

The Gold Standard
of Kings

Kings are owners of property by right of inheritance. They are the masters of their domain. The king owns the realm and everything in it. Those who live in his domain are called subjects. He owns them, in a sense, not as slaves, but as one having authority over them. The subjects are free to leave and find another kingdom to live in. But if they choose to remain, they will be under the governing influence and jurisdiction of the king.

The King James Bible, translated first in 1611 AD, rendered the Hebrew words "Adon" and "Adonay" as Lord. In common terms in England, lords were the landowners. We still use the word "landlord" in our common language today. The Old Testament often used the term Adonay as a name for God, since God was the owner of the planet and everything on it. Over time, the word "lord" has lost its ownership quality and seems to refer to a generic name for God. The new Voice Translation renders over three hundred uses of the term as "owner" rather than "lord." It is refreshing to get back to the real meaning of the word. Over the course of four hundred years, the word has gradually evolved into a much different connotation because of its overuse in the King James Bible.

In the New Testament, the word *"kurios"* was the Greek equivalent to the Hebrew adonay and was rendered "lord." It referred to a person who was an owner. Again, because of overuse through the centuries, "lord" has changed meaning and needs to be updated back to its original intent of referring to God as owner. God was, and is, the original owner and King. He refers to Himself as the "King of Kings." The creator is the owner.

Psalm 24:1–2
The earth is the *Lord's*, and the fulness
thereof; the world, and they that dwell
therein. For he hath founded it upon the seas,
and established it upon the floods.

The Power and Authority of a King

Kings are never voted into power. They are kings by birthright. They determine who they allow in their domain. All power rests in the king. He has the authority over the subjects to expel undesirables from the realm if they are not to his liking. Jesus illustrated that in His parable concerning the unprofitable servant. Talents, or parcels of land, were allotted to three servants for them to produce back for the good of the kingdom. The king was sharing his wealth and property. One of the servants produced nothing and complained that the king did not do any of the work himself, but used the labor of others. The unprofitable servant was deprived of the land that had been allotted to him and "cast into outer darkness." He was told to go find another king whom he could serve; this king would not tolerate his attitude.

Matthew 25:30
And cast the unprofitable servant into outer
darkness:
there shall be weeping and gnashing of teeth.

The King's Word Is Law

The king's authority is absolute. There is no appealing the king's decisions; there is no one to appeal to. The king's words are law. When you understand that Jesus is King and have acknowledged His position, your attitude to the scriptures changes. Now, the words of Jesus take on new authority. They become more important than any other. Now you can see the value in a red-letter edition of the Bible. Now, His words are law, and all the rest of scripture, inspired as it is, becomes commentary and support documents to the King's foundation. There is no greater prophet than Jesus. There is no greater person than Jesus. There is no greater king than Jesus. There is no greater preacher, evangelist, teacher, rabbi, leader, ruler, follower, miracle worker, physician, healer, prayer, or person than Jesus. There was never a day Jesus was not a king. There is no equal to him.

It is easy to see why so many denominations exist. It is because they lost the central leadership position of Jesus as King. They began to follow Paul, James, or John rather than Jesus. Paul said, "Be ye followers of me even as I am of Jesus" (1 Corinthians 11:1). In other words, I follow Jesus, so that is who you should follow. He did *not* say to follow Paul, but to do as he did — follow Jesus. The reformation is built on the letters of Paul and not on the words of Jesus. No wonder it splintered into hundreds of denominations and was unable to get back to the Kingdom concept. Paul is so misinterpreted, just as Peter warned (2 Peter 3:15–16). Keep in mind, all the writers, even though inspired, showed their personality in their writings. Paul's background as a former Pharisee comes through in the complexity of his arguments. Use Paul as a commentary about Jesus. If you ground yourself in the teachings of Jesus, Paul will make perfect sense and be supportive of Jesus's foundation. If you manufacture doctrines out of Paul's writings, you have passed into the world of the Pharisees.

The King Is the Government of the Realm

When John the Baptist declared, "The kingdom of God is at hand," he was saying, and they all understood, "Look around; the king is here; he has arrived." If the king is here, so is the government. In kingdoms, the government travels with the king. Wherever the king goes, so goes the government. Jesus was born a king. He died a king. Every day that He walked the earth, He was a king. Every day before He came and every day after He left, He was and is and forever will be a king. He is the head of the government of heaven, His Kingdom.

The King's Wealth

A king's wealth is measured by the value of property in the realm. Real estate is not the only measure of his wealth; the prosperity of his citizens is also a measure of his wealth and his benevolence. The king's wealth is common in a benevolent kingdom. Not sharing his wealth usually leads to a poorer, unpleasant kingdom. Rehoboam, Solomon's son, was a good example of a king who put himself first and his citizens last. The result was the loss of ten tribes who rebelled and left his kingdom and formed another.

The king's citizenry represents his glory. A good king takes good care of his citizens, helps them prosper, and, in turn, all prosper including the king. The queen of Sheba commented on Solomon's servants, noting they were well cared for:

1 Kings 10:4–5 (NIV)

When the queen of Sheba saw all the wisdom
of Solomon and the palace he had built,
the food on his table, the seating of his
officials, the attending servants in their robes,
his cupbearers, and the burnt offerings he
made at the temple of the *Lord*,
she was overwhelmed.

God's Gold Standard of Kings

Daniel's Prophetic Image

Daniel 2:37–38 (ESV)

You, O king, are a king of kings: for the God
of heaven has given you a kingdom, power,
and strength, and glory. And wheresoever
the children of men dwell, the beasts of the
field and the fowls of the heaven has he given
into your hand, and has made you ruler over
them all. *You are the head of gold.*

Daniel was asked by King Nebuchadnezzar to tell him what dream he dreamed and interpret its meaning. Daniel told the king that his dream was of a statue whose head was of fine gold, his breast and his arms of silver, his belly and his thighs of brass, his legs of iron, his feet part of iron and part of clay. Daniel went on to give the meaning of the statue in the dream. The different metals and parts of the body represented the succession of kingdoms to come on the earth, starting

with the head of gold, which was King Nebuchadnezzar.

We need to explore King Nebuchadnezzar, because God termed him the gold standard of kings. What was it about King Nebuchadnezzar that made him so elevated in honor?

Notice, first, he was called a king of kings in Daniel 2:37. The "a" is very important. He was not *the* King of Kings, but *a* king of kings. There can be only one top King of Kings. That position is reserved for God. But he was a copy of, or type of, king of kings who could illustrate similar attributes that the king of kings possesses. The double use of the word "king" implies that there were kings under him. Indeed, Nebuchadnezzar had conquered a vast area and had brought many kings to Babylon to sit at his table below him as his captives.

But there was one thing that stood out between him and the kings who followed him—he had absolute authority. Whatever the king said was law. He expected everything that he said to be obeyed, even to the degree of demanding that his subjects worship him. The man had absolute power. He needed no votes, no written decrees, just the sound of his voice was law. He threw Shadrach, Meshach, and Abednego in the fiery furnace when they would not bow as he commanded.

King Nebuchadnezzar had been a great king. The king owned everything, but he shared it with his subjects. He had a great city that he had built with their help. The hanging gardens of Babylon are still talked about for their splendor. Everyone in the kingdom was flourishing. Making the king richer meant you were all better off since the king gave you the things that you needed and wanted. King Nebuchadnezzar was very well liked. Under such a king, everyone thrives. He was rough on his enemies, but gracious and giving to his citizens.

The phrase "Oh, King, live forever" would be rightfully desired and said to him. Even more remarkable was his return to power after the seven-year break he suffered during a period of mental illness. God inflicted him with this illness as a way to humble him so that he would acknowledge God as the one above him who gave him his position and power. At the end of his illness, he was restored fully to his position as king. His absolute authority had demanded it. His success as a benevolent king had won him the respect that he needed and deserved. He took care of his subjects, and they took care of him. They managed to care for him during the seven years that he was out of his mind. His kingdom was waiting for his return.

It was his benevolent care of his subjects and absolute power that made him stand out above other kings. The kingdom to follow was not so gifted. King Darius of the Medes and Persian Empire had to make laws and sign them. His word was not good enough. His advisors persuaded him to make a law and sign it contrary to Daniel. It required all, including Daniel, to pray to a god other than the true God. The king liked Daniel and regretted making the law and having to punish Daniel for not keeping it. The king was unable to change the law once he had signed it. His authority was limited by his own laws and lawyers. He had lost a level of authority.

As the image of the statue progresses to the bronze belt, symbolizing Alexander the Great, his authority becomes even less. His men grumbled at the years that they were away from home conquering more lands. "Live forever" would not be a phrase heard in the camps. History records that his brothers and family were poisoned. It has not been proven, but many suspected that Alexander himself may have been killed. When he died, his empire was split up between his generals. He did not have the absolute authority nor the same respect as a gold king.

We are all too familiar with the Roman Empire, whose

kings, or emperors, were in continual struggles to maintain power, often fighting generals from different legions for supremacy. A senate was appointed to aid in the administration of the city of Rome when the emperors were out in battle. That senate gained power as a bureaucracy and later conspired and killed Julius Caesar to prevent him from becoming an emperor.

As we look at the time frame of the image of the statue, we are currently in the age of the feet of clay and iron. We have lost all respect for kings. Most of the world has overthrown their rule. Our lack of respect for authority has taken a toll on our nation. We find it hard to respect our own leaders. Every generation seems to deteriorate into more disrespect. Our country was founded on rebellion to authority. We call it a revolution; Britian calls it a rebellion. Having our own way seems to infect each generation more than the last. Absolute authority vested in one king is far removed from today's reality. Let's blame it on Adam. He started it when he refused to obey the King of Kings.

Singapore's Benevolent Golden Dictator

Singapore is an island city on the tip of the Malay Peninsula. In the year 2023, it was listed as one of the top four cities economically in the world. It also was among the top destinations for tourists. It has been rated one of the top ten cities for the last decade.

But fifty years ago, Singapore was a drug-ridden slum with one of the highest homeless rates in the world. The unemployment rate was among the worst. It would be the last place you would want to visit. What happened in those fifty years? How can a city go from the worst to the best in such a short time?

Between 1819 and 1942, Singapore was a British port used by the East India Trading Company as a drug warehouse. In order to buy China's tea, silk, and gunpowder, East India Trading used opium from Afghanistan to pay for the Chinese goods. They traded Chinese gunpowder to Afghanistan to pay for the opium. China fought two wars, the Opium Wars, trying to stop the inflow of drugs that was wrecking the lives of their people. As a drug port, Singapore was on the receiving end of the worst drug epidemic the world had ever seen.

In 1942, the Japanese occupied the island. In 1945, Singapore became one of the states in the newly created Federation of Malaya. It elected Lee Kuan Yew as its representative in the Malaysian government. Despite last-ditch attempts by Lee Kuan Yew to keep Singapore as a state in the Malaysian union, the Malaysian Parliament, on August 9, 1965, voted 126–0 in favor of the expulsion of Singapore. The parliament cited the poverty, drugs, slums, and lack of jobs on the island which made it impossible for the rest of the country to continue to support the population.

The island was in economic and social collapse. It had one friend, Lee Kuan Yew. He immediately left for Indonesia to try to unite his island with that country, but was turned down. With all avenues of help closed, Lee took over the city as its leader, with the only prospect of hope being their own means to pull the city out of destruction. Lee assumed total authoritarian rule. He was going to have to do the task alone.

Kings are normally rulers by birthright. They ascend to their thrones by way of inheritance. Dictators, on the other hand, are rulers by force. They ascend to their position by way of force, or in Lee's case, by political power.

He immediately outlawed homelessness. If you had no home of your own, you had to live in government housing and pay 25 percent of your income for it. He outlawed joblessness. The unemployed were handed brooms and instructed to sweep the streets. He outlawed chewing gum. If you were caught with it, you were caned (beaten with a stick until you changed your attitude). Some were employed scraping gum off the streets, while others were busy building government housing. But all had to work. He outlawed drugs. Drug dealers were given capital punishment. They were tried immediately. All executions occurred on Saturday of the same week that they were caught.

None of these laws were voted on or discussed. Lee

took over as dictator with the goal of saving his city. Soon, the city began to look better. People were happy to be in shelters. Drugs became impossible to get. The economy started moving forward. A happy, well-cared-for citizenry began working together, unified, and created a world-class city.

On March 23, 2015, Lee died at the age of ninety-one. One hundred seventy million people as well as many world leaders, paid tribute to him. He had overseen Singapore's transformation from a slum to a world-class city with a vibrant economy. It continues to be one of the cleanest cities in the world. He had many critics for his authoritarian rule. He was accused of limiting public protests and curtailing freedom of the press. But those who were willing to examine the results credited him as a benevolent dictator. He was a gold standard of authority. If you have a benevolent ruler, do what he says. It's for your own good. He is looking out for you.

The King of Kings

Jesus will be that king who rules for our good. We may not like all the rules. Adam didn't, and we seem to fit the same mold. But His laws and rules are for our good. The words from His mouth are the words of authority. They are as sharp and compelling as a double-edged sword. He will rule with the force it takes to obtain compliance.

Revelation 19:15

And out of his mouth goes a sharp sword,
that with it he should smite the nations: and
he shall rule them with a rod of iron: and he
treads the winepress of the fierceness and
wrath of Almighty God.

If God's standard of a Golden King is absolute authority, then there is no voting on His decrees. Whatever
the king says is law. That changes the Sermon on the
Mount. It is no longer a sermon, but a set of decrees
and laws to be followed and obeyed.

Notice, in the King James Version of the Bible, which
tends to hide the Kingdom, there are paragraph titles
added by the editors. The titles are not part of scriptures but represent the opinions and viewpoints of the
editors or translators. At the start of Matthew chapter
5, the title added is "Sermon on the Mount." Jesus
spoke to a crowd on a mountainside. The message that
He gave continues for three chapters and ends with the
statement, "they were astonished at his instruction because he taught them as one having authority." Of
course, He sounded authoritative. He was the King,
and these were not suggestions, but decrees.

The editors who do not see the Kingdom, because they
were blind to its existence, titled it a sermon. If you
have the Kingdom in view, you would not call it
"Sermon on the Mount." You would title this section

"Kingdom Law" or "Decrees of the King." The translators and editors of the King James Bible had just transitioned out of the Roman Universal Religion. Over the thousand years of Roman domination, the Kingdom had been hidden and stamped out as much as possible. People who did not accept the Roman religion, but followed Jesus and the Way, were hunted down and killed. These translators were not able to correctly title the sections of scripture, because they never understood the Kingdom. The Roman government never stopped persecuting Kingdom Christians; they just changed how and who did the dirty deeds. The government had thrown them to lions as revolutionaries. But now, one of the government agencies, the Universal Religion, burned them at the stake as heretics.

The best Bibles that you can get are red-letter editions. They put the words of Jesus in red print and distinguish them from the rest of the text. A red-letter edition calls attention to the words of Jesus as being more important. They are. He is King. His decrees are law. I once had a pastor tell me that he could not diminish Paul and his writings, but he could not see that he was diminishing the words of Jesus. To make them equal with other scripture is to diminish them. He didn't understand the authority of gold-standard kings. He was obviously a follower of Paul and not Jesus. Paul is a commentary on the faith. His words are scripture and extremely important, but they must be placed behind the teaching of Jesus. Only use Paul to help you understand Jesus. Read and concentrate on the Gospels before you go beyond. If you get Jesus and His decrees down solid in your mind, you will not be led astray by the current misunderstandings of Paul's writings. If you understand the Kingdom Jesus delivered and taught, the apostle Paul makes perfect sense. Read Paul again with the Kingdom in mind. You will find his writing refreshing and supportive of King Jesus.

If Jesus and Paul were here in the room with us, who would you want to speak? Would you ask Paul to sit down and be quiet while we hear the King? After the King spoke, would we turn to Paul and say, "What did he say?" I know Paul would be as quiet as we when we stand before the throne. If there appears to be a conflict between what Jesus said and what Paul wrote, go with Jesus. It's a no-brainer.

CHAPTER 5

Living in a Kingdom vs. Practicing a Religion

The Kingdom and religion are two different concepts. They are not in the same ballpark. There is a great deal of difference between them. The Kingdom is God's design. Religion is man's design. Kingdoms are a form of government. Religions are a set of rituals and beliefs. Kingdoms are "supply" side economics. Religions are the "demand side." Kingdoms are a top-down, God-governing enterprise. Religions are a bottom-up, man-centered effort.

1st Century Christianity

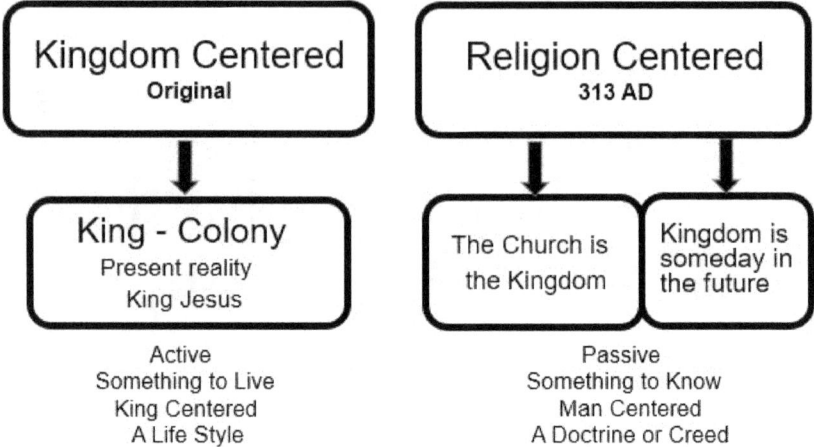

Kingdom Centered Original	Religion Centered 313 AD	
⬇	⬇	⬇
King - Colony Present reality King Jesus	The Church is the Kingdom	Kingdom is someday in the future
Active Something to Live King Centered A Life Style	Passive Something to Know Man Centered A Doctrine or Creed	

God did not promise to make Abraham the founder of a great religion. He promised to make him and his descendants a great nation. Nations are governments ruling over a territory. In that era, all governments were kings with a central city in a territory. The promise covered the territory or realm that God gave to go along with the government of that nation.

Genesis 12:1–2
Now the LORD had said unto Abram,
Get thee out of thy country,
and from thy kindred, and from thy father's
house, unto a land that I will shew thee: and I
will make of thee a great nation,

His descendants turned it into a religion. They wrote a commentary of the Old Testament called the Talmud. Then they built a religious system from that commentary.

Abraham looked for a city owned by God, its maker. That equates to a city whose king is God.

Hebrews 11:9–10
By faith he sojourned in the land of promise, as in a strange country, dwelling in tabernacles with Isaac and Jacob, the heirs with him of the same promise: For he looked for a city which hath foundations, whose builder and maker is God.

The same occurred in Christianity. Jesus brought back the Kingdom, but humans turned it into a religion. The foundation of Christianity is Jesus. The faith must be built on what He said and did as written in the Gospels and early Acts. Many of the denominations of the Reformation are built on the letters of Paul. They diminish the words of Jesus as just stories or parables.

All scripture is given by inspiration, states Paul in his second letter to Timothy. That is true, but you must keep in mind the focal point of its message. The King and the Kingdom take center stage. Which is more important; the promises of the coming King or the actual coming of the King? Whose words are more important; what the King actually said or comments made about what he said after his departure? The center point of scriptures is the Gospels. The Old Testament points ahead to His coming. HE CAME. Then, the New Testament points back to his accomplishments. Jesus is the center. Where can you find him? The Gospels.

There are around two hundred forty-seven denominations. The original mother of them was the Roman Universal Religion, an amalgamation of many religions with the rituals and practices of ten other religions renamed to make them acceptable to Christians. It was termed universal, translated "katholikos" in Greek and "catholic" in English, not because it encompassed all Christians, but rather it encompassed all the religions of Rome. It is the epitome of the word religion. It is full of ceremony, religious garb, chants, and creeds.

In the 1500s, the reformers built their theology on the books of the Bible known as the Epistles, or letters. They did not use the Gospels as their foundation. The Reformation failed to return the faith to the Kingdom because they minimized the four Gospel books. They built their systems of doctrine on the letters of the apostle Paul. The Jewish faith had done the same. Jews built their system on the commentary called the Talmud rather than on the Torah, the actual scriptures. The reformers based their doctrine on the Epistle books and not the Gospels.

The New Testament letters of Paul, Peter, James, and John are great letters and are valuable to have as part of scripture. But when their words are accepted as perfect, while the words of Jesus are blatantly ignored,

Peter's warning comes to life. Many consider Jesus's message to be parables or stories. His Kingdom message delivered on a mountainside is termed a sermon. How long and to what extent do you remember sermons? What did your pastor preach on three weeks ago? Jesus's words are marginalized, while Paul's are extolled. That is exactly why one would miss the Kingdom. If we fail to recognize the kingly position of Jesus, the Kingdom is out of our understanding.

Peter warned about using Paul's letters as a foundation, because they are easily misunderstood and misapplied. Paul's writing came later and is a commentary on the Gospels. They are used to clarify the foundation. Don't use them as the foundation, because they expand on partial concepts to explain things, not to build doctrine on. The Gospels contain the large stones of truth that we need to build a foundation. The Epistles contain the vast number of small bricks that it takes to build the walls. They are both important, but don't build until the foundation is firm.

Jesus is the greatest prophet who ever lived, surpassing even Elijah. Jesus is the greatest law-giver who ever lived, exceeding Moses. Jesus is the greatest miracle worker, eclipsing Elisha. Jesus is the greatest speaker, outshining King Solomon. Jesus is the greatest King, transcending Adam and all subsequent human kings. Anchor yourself on the Jesus found in the Gospels, not on the commentaries.

2 Peter 3:15—16 (TLB)

And remember why he is waiting. He is giving us time to get his message of salvation out to others. Our wise and beloved brother Paul has talked about these same things in many of his letters. Some of his comments are not easy to understand, and there are people who are deliberately stupid, and always demand some unusual interpretation—they have twisted his letters around to mean something quite different from what he meant, just as they do the other parts of the Scripture—and the result is disaster for them.

Kingdoms are easy to live in. It is easy to be an American citizen. We live the American way of life daily without much thought. Just be a law-abiding citizen, and you will have all the privileges of citizenship. As a dual citizen, it is easy to similarly live the Kingdom life and obey its laws, making you a law-abiding citizen of the Kingdom.

Religion, on the other hand, is hard work. You are a member and not a citizen. You have no rights, only obligations. When you join a religious group, they will give you a list of things they expect of you. You will need to attend, give, serve, meet the moral code that they define, and agree with their interpretation of scripture.

In a kingdom, the king takes care of you as a valuable

asset to his realm. The king is the first to give, not the citizen. He hands out parcels of land, or other assets, for the servant to manage and produce abundance to return to the kingdom. The king is center stage and promoted. The more that he thrives, the more he has to share with the citizens. The king also protects and cares for his citizens. In a religion, the members care for the institution. The institution is the receiver, and the members are the givers. The opposite is true in a Kingdom. The King is the giver. He must be, because he is the only one who owns anything.

The Kingdom of God vs. the Kingdom of Heaven

The scriptures contain two phrases, the Kingdom of God and the Kingdom of Heaven. Some believe they are used interchangeably. Those who hold such a position do not have a view of the Kingdom. They see the Kingdom as something in the future, or that the church is the Kingdom. They see Jesus using both terms, so they are unable to distinguish between them. But if they understood the colony concept of governing, they would be able to separate the two.

The Kingdom of Heaven is the place where the King of Kings reigns supreme in person. Because the king is the sole authority in the kingdom, wherever the king is, there is the seat of government. The Kingdom of Heaven is located wherever the King is.

The Kingdom of God is not the same as the Kingdom of Heaven. The Kingdom of God is used to refer to the colony. The King of Kings does not have His throne in that location, but He still rules over the territory. The seat of government is elsewhere, but, nonetheless, the colony is part of His realm. It will help scriptural understanding to have these two terms defined properly. Wherever the King is, is the Kingdom of Heaven. When He moves locations, so moves the seat of government. The colonies never move, but the King does.

If the Kingdom is not understood, the terms become synonymous, since Jesus used both. It confuses those who are blind to the Kingdom, because God came to earth in a body, Jesus, and the Kingdom of Heaven moved with him. Jesus used both terms when He was here on earth because He could. He was the King, and He was here in the colony. During that time, the colony was the same as the seat of government. He returned to heaven and rules from there presently. He will come here again in the future and rule from earth in what is called the Millennial Reign. You can see how confusing it would be to those who don't understand the colony concept of kingdoms. The Kingdom of Heaven moves with the King, while the colony, the Kingdom of God, is static.

CHAPTER 6

Kingdom Lost

The Edict of Milan

In 313 AD, Constantine issued the Edict of Milan. Those blind to the Kingdom hail the edict as the end of persecution for Christians. They extol Constantine as the first Christian emperor. Nothing could be further from the truth. Calling it a lie would be a better characterization. History is full of false storytellers—the victors of every battle tell their version, while the losers are usually dead, with not much to say.

Constantine never converted to Christianity; he fabricated a new form of Christianity to fit his requirements of a religion that would not threaten his empire. The Roman Empire was struggling and threatening to break up because of the Kingdom of God's influence. Like leaven in bread, as Jesus's parable had predicted, His Kingdom was growing and affecting the entire empire as well as regions beyond. Some provinces had given up slavery while others had not. The differences between the Christian community and the other religions began to divide the empire. In order to save the empire, Constantine gave up on the feed-them-to-the-lions method and instituted a new plan. The empire had ten major religions, a dozen minor religions, and the Kingdom of God all competing against one another. He devised an ingenious plan to come up with one combined, amalgamated religion. There would be no divisions. If one new religion could be invented that absorbed all the different religions, the empire could survive. The internal spiritual wars would end.

Constantine invented a single, universal religion for all, which became known as the Roman Universal Religion. In Latin, it was Religio Universala Romana. Notice, it is not the name of a denomination you immediately think of. It was termed a religion. The word "church" did not exist until the 1300s. This new religion incorporated elements from all the religions of the empire and mixed their practices together. Those celebrated pagan religious days would now have Christian names applied to them.

The Kingdom Christians had no buildings or gathering centers since they met in homes. Having a public meeting place would have exposed them to Rome's persecutions. They met regularly for the purpose of education and fellowship. They did not have formal worship services, as seems to be a requirement of present-day culture. The new universal religion needed worship sites. The pagan gods all had temples. Many of those temples were remodeled into buildings with baptistries and altars that reflected the new religious ceremonies to fulfill the obligations of this new religion.

The Edict of Milan was issued to stop any persecution of the separate deities and sects of this new religion. It was now to be one religion with all gods represented. It was not issued to protect Christianity; it was issued to stop Christians from condemning and criticizing the other religions. It was issued to bring unity and forbid any one religion from attacking another in the new all-encompassing religion. The universal religion now incorporated all the people of the empire within its membership and all the various practices. No matter what god they had worshiped, they were now a member of something associated with Christian names. Constantine would claim to be a member of the Roman Universal Religion even though his particular god was Apollo, the sun god.

Although no copies of the edict can be found, some summaries of those who saw it exist. One such summary is quoted in Lactantius's *De mortibus persecutorum (On the Deaths of the Persecutors)*. It is written in Latin around 316 AD and translated as follows:

When we, Constantine Augustus and Licinius Augustus, met so happily at Milan, and considered together all that concerned the interest and security of the State, we decided to grant to everybody the free power to follow the religion of their choice, in order that all that is divine in the heavens may be favorable and propitious towards all who are placed under our authority.

Now the Roman Universal Religion was official, and any criticism of it was deemed heretical by the state and its new religious agency. With the emperor as leader or king of the religion, it became a department of the government. It was the state religion. To speak against the new religion was to violate the emperor's decree issued in the Edict of Milan. Notice his quote in the second line of the edict; the emphasis is on the "interest and security of the state." There was no heart-felt love of God motivating him.

The newly invented religion was intended to replace the Kingdom concept. It would gather the masses of people of the empire into a single cultural belief system. Many Kingdom Christians did not join this new conglomeration of rituals. Before the invention of the Roman Universal Religion, those adherents to the Kingdom were fed to the lions. After the invention, the Kingdom followers were burned at the stake as heretics instead of being cat food. They were smoked rather than devoured. For the next thousand years, Kingdom

Christians would remain in the shadows, this time persecuted by a religious monster capable of killing those who would not accept its dogmas.

Constantine was far from a believer in Christ. On his deathbed, he asked to be baptized just in case Christianity had some truth to it. During his life, he built monuments mostly to himself or Apollo. In his arch of triumph built in Rome to commemorate his victory at the battle of Milvian Bridge, no Christian symbols were etched into its stone, but Apollo and two other gods were represented.

There is only one Christian story told of him. It was concocted two decades after the fact. He supposedly dreamed of a cross in the sky with the words, "You shall conquer in this sign." First of all, this story was told twenty years after the Battle of the Milvian Bridge where it was supposed to have occurred. Second, no reference to a Christian cross ever appeared on any of the monuments he personally designed to commemorate that battle. The story was obviously concocted by those after his life who wanted to portray him as Christian. He was only Christian in the sense that Christian tenets were mingled into the universal religion with his worship of Apollo.

History is full of those who twist the truth for their own gain. To add to the story's audacity, who would believe the cross is a symbol of conquering? The cross, at that time, was a symbol of capital punishment. The

Way used a symbol of a fish for nearly three hundred years to mark some of their meeting places. It came from Jesus's statement that He would make them "fishers of men." To further dispel the fable, Jesus was a pacifist who advocated loving your enemy and not conquering with a sword. He also put forth that the Kingdom was like leaven that would win from within quietly and silently, as yeast works to raise bread. It is still working its internal miracle today.

The Ante-Nicene Writers vs. Saint Augustine

Bible colleges and the seminaries of almost all denominations use Saint Augustine as the source and final authority on ecclesiology or the doctrine of the church. They claim him to be the earliest writer they can find who gives them the history and practices of the church.

Timeline

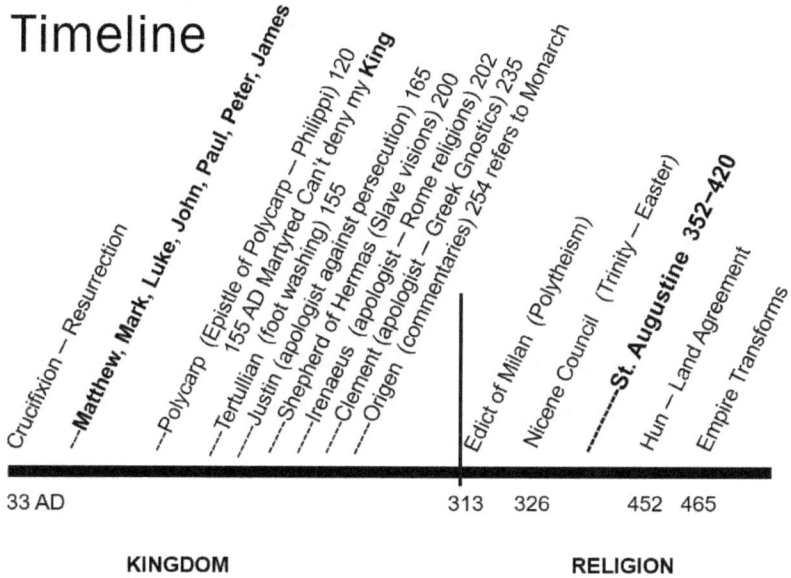

Crucifixion – Resurrection

Matthew, Mark, Luke, John, Paul, Peter, James

Polycarp (Epistle of Polycarp – Philippi) 120

155 AD Martyred Can't deny my **King**

Tertullian (foot washing) 155

Justin (apologist against persecution) 165

Shepherd of Hermas (Slave visions) 200

Irenaeus (apologist – Rome religions) 202

Clement (apologist – Greek Gnostics) 235

Origen (commentaries) 254 refers to Monarch

Edict of Milan (Polytheism)

Nicene Council (Trinity – Easter)

St. Augustine 352-420

Hun – Land Agreement

Empire Transforms

| 33 AD | 313 | 326 | 452 | 465 |

KINGDOM   **RELIGION**

Saint Augustine was born in 352 AD, thirty-nine years after the Edict of Milan. His entire perspective evolved from only having been a part of the universal, state-sanctioned, organization. He never saw or experienced the Kingdom. He only knew and lived life under the universal religion. He lived in Hippo Regius (now Annaba, Algeria), and was a prolific writer who left us over five million words describing the church, its doctrine, and its practices. Those manuscripts are all about the new universal religion, not the Kingdom. By the time he reached adulthood, the Kingdom had been buried out of sight for a half-century.

The theologians in these seminaries and denominations make the assertion that earlier writings of the church have been lost. The truth is they were never written, because there was no church to write about before 313 AD. We have lots of writers and manuscripts from those first three centuries. None of them mention the church or a religious organization. They all use words that are more descriptive of a government organization. They make reference to the king and the monarch. Before the Edict of Milan, the believers functioned as a kingdom. After the invention of the Religio Universala Romana, the face of Christianity took on a religious organizational structure.

How can you say that you lost the works of the early writers when you have the best of them in the Bible itself? The most valuable of these writers are those found in the New Testament. Read again Matthew, Mark, Luke, and John. See if you find the Kingdom coming at you on every page. How could you have missed it? We can be a witness to our own blindness, as we all believed the story given to us that the Kingdom was far ahead in the future, waiting for Jesus to return. How many of us thought that the church is the Kingdom and we are automatically in it because we are in the church? We do not know how we missed it, but Jesus indicated that it has been hidden and hard to find. His parables were all about the Kingdom.

Matthew 13:35
That it might be fulfilled which was spoken
by the prophet, saying, I will open my mouth

in parables; I will utter things which have
been kept secret from the foundation of the
world.

The early followers of the Way, having no buildings or
religious structures, were at the mercy of the new religion. The public image of Christianity was assumed by
Constantine and those he controlled in Rome while the
Way remained in the shadows. Constantine stepped in
and began to call council meetings to set doctrine and
ceremonies. He began to assimilate Christianity into
the universal religion. For example, Ishtar, the goddess
of fertility, had a feast day in April that was set by the
cycles of the moon. It does not always match the Jewish
Passover, since that is set by the Jewish calendar. This
day used rabbits and eggs as symbols of fertility. Since
the Christians had only a couple of days important to
them, such as the resurrection day honored on April 1,
the new universal religion combined the days into one
and called it Easter, which is derived through translations
from the word Ishtar. Have you ever wondered how
Easter bunnies and colored eggs became associated with
the resurrection day?

We don't want to get sidetracked into controversy,
because so many of these pagan practices are ingrained
in our culture after 1,700 years. Many devout Christians
have found ways to explain them and accept them. It
would behoove us just to mention a few of the Roman

gods. Venus and Cupid come to mind. Not only do they spawn Valentine's Day, but they also represent the old Babylonian pagan worship of a mother and child. Do you see why Mary became so important in Christian culture?

Try to explain the demonic day of Halloween and the practice of some churches to hold a "trick or treat" event on their property. There will be those who justify it.

Most readers will be too young to remember that, until the 1970s our public schools only served fish on Friday, because the day was in honor of Dagon, the fish god. Over the centuries, the church found ways to better describe it. They called it meatless Friday. It was officially abolished in 1983 by the Roman Church. Speaking of the fish god, have you seen a church official wear a hat that resembles a fish head?

Rome celebrated the birthday of Apollo, the sun god, on December 25th. On the Julian calendar used for 1,500 years, December 25th was the winter solstice, the day the sun began its journey to rise higher in the sky. Now, you know why Christmas falls on that day, even though shepherds would never have been with their flocks in the fields at that time of year.

It was Constantine himself, a devote follower of Apollo the sun god, who changed the day of rest from Saturn-Day to Apollo's day, known to us as Sun-Day.

Christians have devised many excuses for the change from the seventh day of rest to the first, but check the day it changed and who ordered it. God said the seventh day was the day of rest, the emperor said Sun-Day. See the power of kings. Did you notice your weekdays are all named for Roman gods? Thor-Day is not named by accident. And Moon-Day should be a favorite of the religion that has a crescent on their flag. Ezekial 8:14 mentions the pagan practice of forty days of weeping for Tammuz, a pagan god who died young. That forty-day period ended up in the new universal religion as Lent.

Cultural traditions are hard to break after centuries of observation. Oh, so sorry to mention that word "tradition." Just because it has been done for centuries does not make it right. I refer you to Jesus for His opinion. He is the only one you have to justify yourself to.

CHAPTER 7

Reformation Blues

For the next thousand years, termed the Dark Ages, the scriptures were kept from the public. Since the new universal religion was nothing like the text of the Bible, it was deemed necessary to keep the scriptures hidden.

It was in 1517 when Martin Luther, a Catholic monk in Germany who had access to the Bible manuscripts, noticed there were stark contrasts between church doctrine and scripture. He used Romans 1:17, "The just shall live by faith," to make the case that salvation was by faith and not by church membership, which was the belief held by the universal religion.

Luther argued for salvation based on faith alone. He translated the Bible into German and actually added the word "alone" to his first version of that passage. He did not like the books of James, Hebrews, and the three Gospels of Matthew, Mark, and Luke. Those books stress the evidence of a changed life as critical to salvation. He advocated for the deletion of these books from the canon of scriptures.

Following Luther's lead, other reformers took over as they began to dig more deeply and interpret the scriptures differently. John Calvin put forth the doctrine of election and salvation by theology. It was not faith, but God's choice that saved you. You were destined to heaven by divine selection. Oh yes, faith was present, but you came to faith because God chose for you.

The Anabaptists were the last name used by Kingdom Christian groups and is still in use today. They are distinct in their version of Christianity as having a king and a separate citizenship. Don't mistake them as Baptist; they are not the same. Baptists are strong on adherence to the scriptures but fail to have a king or separate citizenship. They do share the same view on baptism by immersion after salvation, but as a whole, Baptists do not hold to a literal present kingdom. Baptists came through the reformation, while Anabaptists, meaning re-baptizers, never left the Kingdom concept. They were part of the groups from the Dark Ages that continued to live as citizens of the Kingdom of God. Kingdom groups, including Anabaptists, were persecuted through the ages as heretics having held to the Kingdom principles of the Gospel. They declared themselves to be citizens of another nation, the Kingdom of God. On the other hand, Reformation Christians were persecuted in their early history only because they represented change and rebellion against the leader hierarchy. Even though the reformation made many positive changes, most failed to go as far as restoring the Kingdom Gospel that Jesus delivered.

Anabaptists trace their heritage back to the lion arenas and burning stakes. If you search the Internet for information on them, you will find information about the Kingdom. They still have it. Non-Kingdom authors don't understand their position and write in general about them. But if you get the writings of the Anabaptists themselves, you will find the Kingdom. It is best to go to the source rather than what others say about them.

† The Kingdom

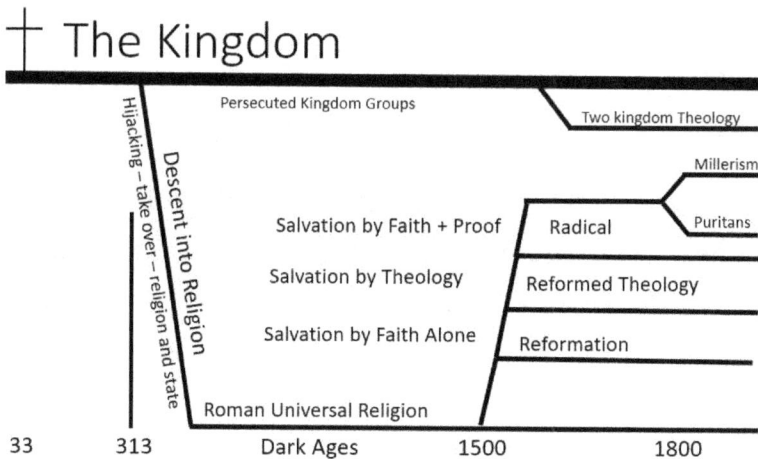

	Persecuted Kingdom Groups		Two kingdom Theology
			Millerism
Salvation by Faith + Proof	Radical	Puritans
Salvation by Theology	Reformed Theology	
Salvation by Faith Alone	Reformation	
Roman Universal Religion		

Hijacking – take over – religion and state
Descent into Religion

| 33 | 313 | Dark Ages | 1500 | 1800 |

Radicals took over the reformation as time went on. They held the concept of works, or how you live and perform the Christian faith, as an important part of salvation. They emphasized salvation by faith, but concluded there had to be proof by a changed life for that faith to be real.

Paul had been a Pharisee, a religious lawyer. His attention to detail comes through his writings. The reformers constructed doctrine from Paul's letters and failed to hear the clarion call from the lips of the King that our focus should be the Kingdom. Since they viewed Jesus as a child, they counted the words of Paul as more important than those of Jesus. The introduction of the Roman religion of a mother and child, Venus and Cupid, influenced the lowering of the authority of Jesus. It is not a surprise that they used Paul more than Jesus in their intellectual pursuits; a classic case of missing the forest for the trees. If you have ever been lost in a forest, you know the value of a helicopter in order to get the long view.

Overall, the Reformation and the denominations that it spawned failed to return Christianity to the Kingdom level of living. Because they centered on doctrine and Paul's letters, avoiding Jesus's teachings in the Gospels, they were unable to find the King and His domain. It is time to complete the efforts of the Reformation and move into the Kingdom. There is work yet to be done.

There are challenges to meet and obstacles to overcome. The reformation will not be complete until the Kingdom is restored and preached.

What is the heart of the controversy? How can we summarize the issue and make it simple to understand? There is just one question: do you have a King? If you hold Jesus to be your King, then you are His domain and you are in the Kingdom. It behooves you to start living under the King's authority. If you hold to the belief that Jesus will someday come to be a King, then you have no King presently and you are not in a Kingdom. If you believe the church is the Kingdom, yet it does not recognize Jesus as King, it is a kingless organization and definitely not the Kingdom it claims to be.

It remains our task to find a way to get the church culture to see and somehow gain insight into the present-day Kingdom. Living a Kingdom life makes Christianity easy to live and understand. It removes the work and obligations and puts the joy of the abundant life within reach. How can we help the church and its people find the promised land that God has for them? The present-day church struggles in the wilderness having never reached the promise land of the Kingdom.

Originally, Jesus's followers were not of this world, but citizens of another. The Romans took Christianity and turned it into a government agency. The Greeks turned it into a philosophy. Europe turned it into a culture. But in America, we have turned Christianity into a business. May God forgive us. If we can ground our faith in Jesus and His teachings, we will be Kingdom-centered as He was. Then and only then could we have unity, as there is but one King and one leader, Jesus.

If you have one leader, you have unity. Having just a king, first-century followers had unity. But putting the detailed lawyer, Paul, above the King led to two hundred forty-seven denominations and counting. They have to ignore much of what Jesus said to hold to many of their doctrines. They count Jesus's words as sermons rather than law. They hold His words as things to think about, not obey.

Doctrinal issues are not God's priority. His goal is to get you into the Kingdom. That is number one for Him. He is not concerned about what you know, but who you know. In the parable of the ten virgins found in Matthew 25, scholars argue what the oil represents. Some say it's to fill your lamp with wisdom or knowledge. Some say it's the filling of the Holy Spirit. They both miss the point of the parable. It is a simple matter of having prepared for who is coming, no matter what the oil is. Have you prepared for the right groom who is coming to the wedding? The true thrust of the parable is the groom, not the oil. Whatever the oil is does not matter, as long as you have prepared sufficiently for who you think is coming. If you think the groom is your friend, you may not have prepared much and be dressed casually. Or maybe you were expecting a rich man, so you dressed well. You might have anticipated the President of the United States and worn a tuxedo. What if you were wrong? What if a king is coming to His wedding? Have you seen a royal wedding? The daylong event takes extreme preparation. You will need your royal attire and the fanciest top hat. Ladies will need formal dresses and the most glorious hat that they can buy.

You see how the arguments of these scholars are trivial. They will miss the King when He comes because they have missed Him now. Many groups have degraded into trivial pursuits. It does not matter what the oil in your lamp represents as much as it matters for whom you have prepared. Be ready to meet a king.

Proof that God's priority is your good conduct more than your knowledge is Jesus's parable about His Kingdom and the final arbitration. It is not what you believed about doctrines, but how much you loved and obeyed Him. He said, "If you love me, keep my commandments." How do you demonstrate that love? After all, the King said, "A new *commandment* I give unto you: that you love one another."

Matthew 25:32–46 (MKJV)
And before him shall be gathered all nations:
and he shall separate them one from another,
as a shepherd divides his sheep from the
goats:
And he shall set the sheep on his right hand,
but the goats on the left.
Then shall the King say unto them on his
right hand, Come, you blessed of my Father,
*inherit the kingdom prepared for you from the
foundation of the world*:
For I was hungry, and you gave me meat: I
was thirsty, and you gave me drink: I was a
stranger, and you took me in:
Naked, and you clothed me: I was sick, and
you visited me: I was in prison, and you came
unto me.
Then shall the righteous answer him, saying,
Lord, when did we see you hungry and feed
you? or thirsty, and give you drink?
When did we see you a stranger, and take
you in? or naked, and clothe you?
Or when did we see you sick, or in prison,
and come unto you?
And the King shall answer and say unto
them, Verily I say unto you,
*inasmuch as you have done it unto one of the least
of these my brethren, you have done it unto me.*

Then shall he say also unto them on the left
hand, depart from me, you cursed, into
everlasting fire, prepared for the devil and his
angels:
For I was hungry, and you gave me no meat:
I was thirsty, and you gave me no drink:
I was a stranger, and you took me not in:
naked, and you clothed me not: sick, and in
prison, and you visited me not.
Then shall they also answer him, saying,
Lord, when did we see you hungry, or
thirsty, or a stranger, or naked, or sick, or in
prison, and did not minister unto you?
Then shall he answer them, saying, Verily I
say unto you,
inasmuch as you did it not to one of the least of
these, you did it not to me.
And these shall go away into everlasting
punishment: but the righteous into life
eternal.

Theological Divisions

One of the current-day views of Reformation theology
is called dispensationalism. It divides the Bible into
time periods and asserts that scripture pertaining to
certain time periods do not apply to you. That
interpretation puts forth that we are in the church age,
so the Old Testament is only an example and does not

apply to us. We can learn from those scriptures, but we don't live under them. They have seven different time periods laid out. They say the church age, our current time period, began at Pentecost, which is chapter 2 of the book of Acts. They conclude all of what Jesus says in the Gospels happens in a different time period, the end of Old Testament. They view Jesus with less relevance than Paul. They say we can learn from Jesus, but his message is the culmination of the age of the "law." They fail to elevate the importance of His words.

They ignore the Gospel that Jesus preached, the Good News that you can be born again and live life in the Kingdom under the care of the King. They teach a partial Gospel of being born again or redeemed from sin and wait till you get to heaven to receive the bounty. Theirs is a life of trials. The Kingdom life is an adventure in victories. Their goal is some time in the future. Jesus's message is for the here and now. If your primary citizenship is here on this earth in a republic, I am sorry for your struggle. But if your primary citizenship is in the Kingdom of God, you are under the authority and care of a very capable King.

Jesus said:

> Matthew 24:35
> Heaven and earth shall pass away,
> but *my* words shall not pass away.

He did not say the scriptures would not pass away. He did not say Paul's words would not pass away. He said *His words* would not pass away. The words of Jesus should never be disregarded or diminished. He did say "follow *me*." How can you follow without knowing what He said? Dispensationalism, along with all the other "isms," is a distraction that hides the Kingdom from you. Leave "salvation-by-theology" behind and keep going toward the Kingdom.

Matthew 6:33 (DRA)
Seek ye therefore first the kingdom of God,
and his justice, and all these things shall be
added unto you.

Seek the Kingdom first, and be in right standing with its rules and laws. Then the King will take care of you. You will have the King's favor.

CHAPTER 8

Translation Trials

Translations, by their nature, are biased and opinionated. After all, we all have a bias in our lives. Some of us were raised poor, some rich. That gives us a framework from which we see the world. Some of us were healthy, some not so much, some tall, some short, some male, some female; some were raised in peace, some in war zones, some in religious homes, some not. We see the world differently because of the environment in which we were raised. We have a history that is unique to ourselves. That history gives us our window through which we see the world. It's our bias that we can try to escape from, but it is very hard to do.

Translations of the Bible are even more prone to bias. Those who get to the level of education that it takes to translate from Greek or Hebrew have gone through various schools to get where they are. Those schools all have a theological philosophy or bend to what they teach. A Presbyterian seminary will give you a different view of the scriptures than a Catholic seminary. A Pentecostal seminary will give you a different view than a Baptist seminary. Translators arrive at the workplace with a particular set of biases that they have picked up along the way. It is not a bad thing, but it is something you need to be aware of as you evaluate the various translations of the Bible. There is great value in using multiple translations so that you get a broad view of word choices. You want those wide views of scripture so that you can obtain every option possible for the most comprehensive insight.

The New Testament is translated from a language that no one speaks today; Konia Greek. That is the Greek used on the streets two thousand years ago. It was common then, but languages change over time. The Greek people today cannot read or understand the Greek spoken at the time of Christ, just as we find the English of 1759, the Authorized King James, to be difficult and awkward. Try the King James of 1611, or perhaps you have read the original works of Chaucer or Shakespeare. I am sure speedreading them is not an easy task.

When you open the dictionary to check a word, you have several descriptive phrases and synonyms to compare. In selecting those synonyms, your bias comes into play. You tend to pick the translation that matches how you view the meaning of those words as they fit your bias. Your meaning will be different than that of others who have a different way of life from yours. People just see things differently. It is impossible to avoid bias. A Catholic with a thousand-year history behind him and trained in that view of Christianity will use different word choices than a person raised in a Protestant setting. Their preset training will give them different choices.

Let's get a concrete example. The King James Bible was translated by seventy Anglican priests under the direction of King James, all with Catholic backgrounds. They had just broken away from the Roman Catholic Church making only one change — the King of England was now head of the church and not the pope. In translating Matthew 16:24, the priests chose the word "deny" for the meaning of the Greek word "aparneomai," as they were accustomed to the Catholic doctrine of denying things for Lent. It was in their training.

Matthew 16:24

Then said Jesus unto his disciples, if any man
will come after
me, let him *deny* himself, and take up his
cross, and follow me.

But in the list of choices under the Greek lexicon is another word, "disown." When you have an understanding of the Kingdom and the ownership rights of the King, disown becomes the obvious choice. To follow Jesus means to let Him be King and *own* you, as in "you are bought with a price" (1 Corinthians 6:20). To use the word "deny" sets a much lower standard, and it eliminates any connection to Kingdom thinking. They chose this word because they did not have Jesus as king, but rather the pope, or King James. Also, the old religious tenet of self-sacrifice as a way to gain favor with God influenced their choice of words. They were accustomed to the pagan practice of Lent used since the time of Augustine to do penance. Somehow, mankind thinks that he can earn his own salvation by way of making some payment.

Young's Literal Translation, published in 1862 by Robert Young, used the Textus Receptus for the basis of his work. It had a Kingdom view that allowed him a different insight into the Greek text.

Matthew 16:24 (YLT)
Then said Jesus to his disciples, "If any one will come after me, let him *disown* himself, and take up his cross, and follow me."

You can see how bias in translations works to hide the Kingdom from your eyes and mind. Young was a member of the Free Church of Scotland that traced its roots back to the apostles and the Kingdom teachings of the early centuries before 313 AD. Ownership is a big word in the scriptures ignored by the common Christian teachings of our day. As Western democracies move further away from kingdoms, they lose the comprehension of commonwealths and king ownership of the realm. In old England, "lord" meant "owner." The houses of lords were the landowners, while the houses of commoners were the renters. *Adonai* and *Kurios* are Greek and Hebrew words that mean "owner" and were translated as "Lord." The Voice translation, published in 2011, correctly replaces more than three hundred instances of the word "Lord" with the word "owner." New translations are bringing us closer to the Kingdom as the characteristics of the King come back to light.

Ekklesia

The first instance of the Greek word "ekklesia" in the historical records was in 621 BC. It was used as a term for the summoned group of citizens in Athens called to a government meeting. It was a government term with no religious connotation.

In 321 BC, Aristotle used the word in his writing about democracy. It was used in the context of a "called out," "selected group," or "assembly" of men who would administer the government. Again, the word was associated with government, not religion.

Ekklesia was translated in 29 BC by the Romans as the word "senate." The Roman Senate was a group of selected, appointed men that held power in conjunction with the emperor. Again, the word was clearly nonreligious and connected to governing.

When a Roman Universal Religion member, Jerome, translated the scriptures into Latin in 382 AD, called the Vulgate, he did not translate the word "ecclesia," but left in the text as a Greek word. The aim of the new Roman religion was not translating words that would not match the practices that they had instituted. Therefore, words like ecclesia that had government connotations were left untranslated. Baptize, which means to immerse under water, was also left in Greek, so the meaning would be ambiguous. The universal religion was practicing baptism by other ways, such as pouring or sprinkling. For the next thousand years, other translations of scripture were forbidden by the Roman Universal Religion.

In 1382, John Wycliffe translated the scriptures into English, that the word "church" was first used. After a thousand years of religious emphasis rather than government concepts, the bias toward a religious word would have been well entrenched. Wycliffe pulled a word out of Gaelic, "kirk," which means religious circles to use for ecclesia. There were many religious circles in the British Isles, Stonehenge being just one example. The term applies to structures as well as people. But by the fourteenth century, religious buildings were well established as symbols of the faith.

The English translation of the Gaelic word kirk is church. The meaning of ecclesia had evolved from a government word into a religious word. That evolution makes it harder for people to find the Kingdom. The whole mindset in our present time is toward religion and not government. We have been trained in religion and have nearly wiped-out kingdoms from the face of the earth. It is no wonder the Kingdom is becoming harder to find, not easier. We have a cultural bias toward republics and democracies.

CHAPTER 9

Prove It

You and I have been selected for jury duty. We are seated in the jury box. Jesus has been charged with the crime of "establishing a kingdom." The judge is giving pre-trial instructions:

Ladies and gentlemen of the jury, attorneys for the plaintiff and defense, this court will accept all first-hand eyewitness accounts of the events in question. Second-hand accounts are considered hearsay and will not be accepted. Many opinions exist as to the history of the early followers of the Messiah, but opinions don't make facts. Current-day pastors and theologians will not be considered because they were not eye-witnesses. They were not present for these events, but have formed opinions based on things they heard or read from others. The testimony and writings of the reformers of the sixteenth century will not be considered. Do not call Martin Luther, Huldrych Zwingli,

John Calvin, Charles and John Wesley to give testimony. They have opinions, but were not present to have first-hand knowledge. They are hearsay witnesses and have no valid claim to facts. St. Augustine and those of the fourth century are also hearsay testimony and cannot be relied on. Please restrict your witnesses to first-hand accounts of those who were eyewitnesses to the events in question. We will assume these witnesses to be sworn in to tell the truth, as most of them were martyred for their statements, unwilling to recant the things they said and wrote.

Court is now in session. Please call your first witness.

Your Honor, I call Zechariah to the stand:

The Testimony of Zechariah and Isaiah

It was God's aim to restore the Kingdom and reestablish man's rule on the planet. The prophets, one-by-one, announced the coming of a new man, a second Adam, the Messiah. He would be the kingly government that God had intended. No wonder the Jewish people looked for a ruler, a king who would set up a kingdom. Today's theologians suggest that the Jewish people were in error to expect such a leader. But these theologians are blind to God's plan for His Kingdom. The Jewish people were correct, on the mark, and in line with what the prophets predicted—a coming king. But they misinterpreted the type of king that they should have expected. They expected a military king, not a benevolent king.

Zechariah 9:9 (ESV)
Rejoice greatly, O daughter of Zion! Shout aloud, O daughter of Jerusalem! Behold, *your king* is coming to you; righteous and having salvation is he, humble and mounted on a donkey, on a colt, the foal of a donkey.

Isaiah 9:6–7
For unto us a child is born, unto us a son is given: and the *government* shall be upon his shoulder: and his name shall be called Wonderful, Counsellor, The mighty God. Of the increase of *his government* and peace there shall be no end, upon the throne of David, and upon *his kingdom*.

The Testimony of John the Baptist

Matthew 11:13
For all the prophets and the law prophesied *until* John.

Even though he appears in the New Testament, John the Baptist has been called the last of the Old Testament prophets by current-day theologians. They point to the prediction of Elijah returning and making straight the paths of the Messiah. But he is not. He is the first of the New Testament truthtellers, proclaiming the predictions of the past are now being fulfilled.

John 1:21 (BBE)
And they said to him, What then? Are you
Elijah? And he said, I am not.
Are you the prophet? And his answer was, I
am not.

Make no mistake: the message of John the Baptist was a Kingdom message. He did not declare a new religion was on the horizon. He did not issue a report about the church's inception. He brought a simple message that the Kingdom was at hand. By announcing the presence of the Kingdom, he was proclaiming the advent of the King.

Matthew 3:1
In those days came John the Baptist, preaching in the wilderness,
And saying, "repent: for the *kingdom of heaven* is at hand."

John the Baptist is not predicting the future; he is pointing to the here and now. The King is on site. The Kingdom is here at last. His message is very different than that of the former prophets. He was to lay out the red carpet for the King to enter upon.

Jesus's Sworn Statements over a Three-Year Period

After the Baptist proclaimed Jesus to be "the lamb of God" and Baptized Him, Jesus picked up the same theme; the Kingdom is here. The Kingdom is available now. He said, "I am here to bring it to you."

Matthew 4:17
From that time Jesus began to preach, "Repent: for the *kingdom* of heaven is at hand." *(The Kingdom is here now.)*

Matthew 4:23
And Jesus went about all Galilee, teaching and preaching the gospel of the kingdom. (Jesus always connected the gospel, or good news, to the Kingdom.)

(Current day Gospel is redemption from sin omitting the Kingdom)

Mark 1:14
After John was put in prison, Jesus came into Galilee, preaching the *gospel of the kingdom of God* . . .

Mark 1:15
The time is fulfilled, and the *kingdom of God* is at hand: repent and believe the good news. *(Jesus always connected the good news to the Kingdom.)*

Luke 4:43

Jesus said, I must preach the *kingdom of God*:
for that purpose, am I sent.

(A major declaration of the plan and purpose
of His coming.)

Matthew 5:3
Blessed *are* the poor in spirit: for theirs is the
kingdom of heaven.

Luke 12:32
Fear not, for it is your Father's good pleasure
to give you the kingdom. (God gave as a free
gift, the Kingdom to Adam, and it is His
intent to extend that gift to us.)

Matthew 6:10
Thy *kingdom* come. Thy will be done in earth,
as *it is* in heaven.

(The Kingdom is to be the first request in our
prayers.)

Matthew 6:13
For thine is the kingdom, and the power, and
the glory, forever. ("Thine" is an ownership
word. In a kingdom, all belongs to the king,
who willingly shares with his subjects.)

Luke 16:16

The law and the prophets were preached
until John: since that time the kingdom of
God is preached. (The Kingdom coming was
preached, but now a new message is given:
the Kingdom is here.)

Matthew 12:28

If I cast out devils by the Spirit of God, then
the *kingdom of God* has arrived.

(Concrete evidence of the presence of the
Kingdom.)

Luke 8:10

To you it is given to know the mysteries of
the *kingdom of God*: but to others in parables;
that seeing they might not see, and hearing
they might not understand. *(Matthew 13:35: "I
will open my mouth in parables; I will utter things
which have been kept secret from the foundation of
the world.") (The Kingdom is the great secret of
the scriptures that man has been blinded to and
cannot easily see. Adam's eyes were opened to the
natural world and closed to the spiritual world.)*

Luke 9:27

There are some standing here, which shall not
taste of death, till they see the *kingdom of God.*
*(The Kingdom would be reestablished in their
lifetime; it is here and now.)*

Matthew 16:19

And I will give unto thee the keys of the
kingdom of heaven . . .

Luke 17:20–21

And when he was asked by the Pharisees,
when the *kingdom of God* should come, he
said, the kingdom of God cometh not with
observation: Neither shall they say, here! or,
there! for the *kingdom of God* is within you.
*(The Kingdom of God is not a visible kingdom,
but, in the heart, an invisible kingdom, a
borderless kingdom.)*

Luke 22:18

Jesus said, I will not drink of the fruit of the
vine, until the *kingdom of God* shall come.

Luke 22:29

I appoint unto you a kingdom, as my Father
hath appointed unto me. (You will be a king,
just as my father has designated me a king.)

Pilate's Recorded Conversation with Jesus *(entered as evidence)* (Exhibit A)

The Jews delivered Jesus to Pilate, accusing him of
claiming to be a king. That was a correct charge. He
was a king and claimed to be so. Pilate satisfied himself
that Jesus was a king, but not a threat to Rome, because
Jesus said that His realm was from far away. There

were many kings under the rule of Rome who posed no threat to the empire, because they governed various territories inside the Roman Empire. So long as Jesus was not trying to take Caeser's place or start a rebellion to break away from the empire, he was welcome to be a king.

John 18:33

Then Pilate entered the judgment hall and called Jesus, and said, "You are the *King of the Jews*?" *(A declarative statement given to elicit a response.)*

John 18:34

Jesus answered, "Do you say this statement of your own belief, or did others tell you?" *(Jesus affirms the statement of His kingship by asking how Pilate came to this truth.)*

John 18:35

Pilate answered, "Am I a Jew? Your own Nation and the chief priests have delivered you to me: what have you done?" *(Pilate declines to answer and changes the subject.)*

John 18:36

Jesus answered, "*My kingdom* is not of this world: if *my kingdom* were of this world, then would my servants fight, that I should not be delivered to the Jews: but now is *my kingdom* from another place. *(I am not trying to take your kingdom; I have my own. Your domain is here on this earth; my domain is from far away or above.)*

John 18:37

Pilate said, "You are a *king* then!" Jesus answered, "You say *I am a king*. To this end was I born, and for this cause came I into the world, that I should bear witness unto the truth." *(The purpose of His coming to earth was to be a king. In that day, it was not a crime to be a king.)*

Jesus's Testimony after the Resurrection

Jesus was back for forty days in a risen, glorified body that could walk through walls and transport itself through space and time. His physical body had changed, but His message had not. He was still proclaiming and preaching the Kingdom. Nothing could derail the purpose for which He had come: to proclaim, win, and reestablish the kingdom once given to Adam.

Acts 1:3

He showed himself alive after his crucifixion, being seen forty days, and speaking of the things pertaining to the kingdom of God. (His message did not change because of the crucifixion. His purpose and message are the same: establish the Kingdom.)

Matthew 24:14
And this gospel of the kingdom shall be preached in all the world for a witness unto all nations; and then shall the end come. (The church's current definition of the gospel is a partial message. It is only the door to the Kingdom. The complete message is, "Here is the door, go through it so you can live in the Kingdom." Living in the Kingdom is the goal. Just going through the door does not guarantee the abundant life of the Kingdom.)

Matthew 28:18
Jesus said, *all power (rule, authority, kingship)* is given unto me in heaven and in earth.

Disciples Testimony after the Ascension

After Jesus departed for heaven and left His followers to carry on, the message was the same; the Kingdom of God is here now and available for you.

Acts 14:21–22
And when they had preached the gospel to that city, and had taught many, they returned again to Lystra, and to Iconium, and Antioch, confirming the souls of the disciples, and exhorting them to continue in the faith, and

that we must through much tribulation enter
into the *kingdom of God*.

Acts 19:8
And he went into the synagogue speaking
boldly for three months persuading them
concerning the *kingdom of God*.

Acts 20:25
I know all of you, among whom I have been
preaching the *kingdom of God*.

(A quote of the apostle Paul.)

Acts 28:30–31
And Paul dwelt two whole years in his own
hired house, and received all that came in
unto him, preaching the *kingdom of God*, and
teaching those things which concern the Lord
Jesus Christ.

Testimony of a Hostile Witness

Most interesting is the evaluation of the opposition.
What did the adversaries understand the message of the
new group to be? What did they convey to the outside
world? Communication is a complex task that can be
difficult. So, a clear statement from an antagonist as to
what they are hearing and objecting to is an important
revelation. This is one of the best sources on what the
message of the early followers was.

Acts 17:7

Whom Jason hath received: and these all do contrary to the decrees of Caesar, saying that there is another *king*, one Jesus.

Acts 17:7 (CEV)

Jason has welcomed them into his home. All of them break the laws of the Roman Emperor by claiming that someone named Jesus is *king*.

Acts 17:7 (Message)

Jason is hiding them, these traitors and turncoats who say *Jesus is king* and Caesar is not!

Acts 17:7 (Voice)

And this man, Jason, has given them sanctuary and made his house a base for their operations. We want to expose their real intent: they are trying to overturn Caesar's sensible decrees. They're saying that *Jesus is king*, not Caesar!

The events in Acts 17 occurred in 49 AD, while Paul was in Thessalonica. The message is still the same twenty years after the crucifixion and resurrection: Jesus is king now. Note that the writings and sayings of Paul are consistent with those of Jesus. Take Jesus's message as a foundation, and Paul's message supports it fully. Paul makes no changes to Jesus's message.

First-Century Witnesses

The New Testament was written between 50 and 95 AD. We have recorded in its pages the inspired writings of the apostles and disciples of Jesus. It is important to note that the message did not change over the course of the decades that followed. The people who took up the mantle *and* task of spreading the good news of the Kingdom did not deviate from that central theme: the Kingdom is here.

Paul on the Kingdom:

Acts 28:30

Paul, stayed two years in his own house and received all that came to him, preaching the *kingdom* and Jesus.

1 Corinthians 4:20

For the kingdom of God is not in word, but in power. (Not in thought or idea, but real and tangible.)

Colossians 1:13

Who has delivered us from the power of darkness, and has translated *us* into the *kingdom* of his dear Son.

Colossians 4:11

They are my fellow workers in the *kingdom of God.*

Hebrews 12:28

We received a *kingdom* which cannot be
moved, that we may serve God acceptably.
*(We have a king now and strive to be citizens in
good standing.)*

Philippians 3:20 (Voice)

But we are citizens of heaven, exiles on earth
waiting eagerly for a Liberator, our Lord
Jesus the Anointed.

James on the Kingdom:

James 2:5

God has chosen the poor of this world rich in
faith, and *heirs of the kingdom*. He promised
the *Kingdom* to those that love him?

Peter on the Kingdom:

1 Peter 2:9

But you *are* a chosen generation, a royal
priesthood, a holy *nation*, a peculiar people;
that ye should show forth the praises of him
who has called you out of darkness into his
marvelous light. *(A nation — not a religion, not a
church; peculiar: citizens, chosen, senators,
ambassadors, children of the kings.)*

John on the Kingdom:

Revelation 1:5

And from Jesus Christ, *who is* the faithful witness, *and* the firstborn of the dead, and the prince of the *kings* of the earth.

Revelation 1:6

And has made us a *kingdom of priests* unto God and his Father; to him *be* glory and *dominion* for ever and ever.

Revelation 1:9

I John, who also am your brother, and companion in tribulation, and *in the kingdom*.

Your Honor, the defense has a thousand more witnesses, but we feel we have proved our case. Our closing arguments are as follow:

Seeing all these verses and hearing all this evidence clarifies for us that the theme of the Gospel is the Good News of the Kingdom. The Gospels and Jesus have a clear message about the King and his Kingdom. While the commentaries of Paul, John, and Peter clarify individual topics, they must not distract us from the major theme of Jesus. When Paul clarifies the Good News of Jesus's death and resurrection, he is expounding on just a part of the Good News, the door to the Kingdom. Jesus wants us going through that door and then occupy the whole room. See the Kingdom beyond the door.

If we take only one statement of Paul that the Gospel is the death, burial, and resurrection, he is not nullifying the entire gospel. He is just pointing out one particular part of it. If we begin a conversation about a table in my home, we would spend much of our time on the topic of the tabletop because it is our contact point. We would see and touch it. It would be the focal point of our conversation, but the top is only a two-dimensional object. The legs make the table three-dimensional and expand its volume. We can chat about the top, but we cannot ignore the legs, which are a major part of the table. Even though we emphasize the top, the whole table is still intact and is just as important.

If I bought a large farm and stood at the gate to look over the area from the entrance, I would fail to occupy and enjoy the land beyond the gate. So, Christians stay at the gate of the Kingdom and sing praises for the way in, but they never enter in and enjoy the land beyond.

Your Honor, The defense rests.

The judge issues his final instructions to the jury:

Ladies and Gentlemen of the Jury, you have heard and seen the evidence. It is your duty to render a verdict as to the claims of Jesus concerning His Kingdom and Kingship.

This is an awesome decision. It is not His life that hangs in the balance, it is yours. How you decide will determine how you live the Christian life for the remainder of the time you are left on this planet.

May God give you wisdom.

CHAPTER 10

What Difference Does It Make?

I was so excited with my newfound citizenship. Every day was fresh with new discoveries. I would share these gems with my wife about the research and the amazing Kingdom truths I found. One day, she asked what difference it made. That was a great question. The differences were profound, but I had to think about how to express it in simple terms.

After some thought, my response was to inquire how it might affect her if we changed her citizenship to Russia, or China. Would that affect your life and the way you live? Everything changes when you change your citizenship. The Kingdom Christian life is so much simpler and easier. The Bible becomes easier to understand, and now it fits together in a single narrative. Being a Christian requires a change in citizenship, a change in governments, and a change in allegiance. To present Christianity in any less form is heresy. The Jesus whom I know is a king of a real functioning kingdom. Find Jesus, acknowledge him as Savior and King, and obey his laws. Simple Simon. Explaining Christianity had never been so easy.

The Kingdom changes your perspective of Jesus.

When you elevate Jesus to His rightful position as King, you are recognizing the message that He brought to the earth. His message was the advent and appearance of the King. The perspective of Jesus as a religious person who started a religion now gives way to a king who established a kingdom. If you miss Jesus as King, you have wasted your life in trivial pursuit. You have missed who He is.

Spiritual growth is the elevation of Jesus in our lives. John the Baptist summarized it best when he said, in John 3:30, "He must increase, I must decrease." More of Him, less of me. You have not reached spiritual maturity until you have raised your opinion of Jesus to equal His true position. Anything less than King is an insult to God. That is what He calls Himself—King of Kings.

Journey to the Promised Land, the Kingdom

Kingdom = King + Domain

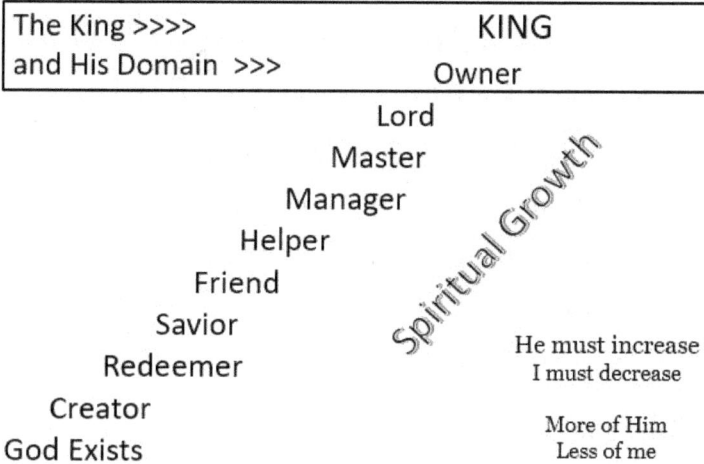

The King >>>>	KING
and His Domain >>>	Owner

Lord

Master

Manager

Helper

Friend

Savior

Redeemer

Creator

God Exists

Spiritual Growth

He must increase
I must decrease

More of Him
Less of me

We must be willing to break the mold and relate to God in a new, higher way. Remember how excited and happy you were when you arrived at the certainty you have a savior? Each time we move up a level in our spiritual growth, we think we have mastered the Christian life. But we find new levels because we don't stop searching. We search because the human heart will not be satisfied until we have arrived at the place God made us for. We were created in His image, and He created us to be like Him. That image flows from the King of Kings down to us as a yearning to find God's best. Setting the goal to reach the Kingdom should have been presented to us immediately when we came to faith. The successful churches of the future will be those that clearly set the target of God's

Kingdom for their people. Those are the churches that are interested in truly helping people grow.

The Kingdom changes your perspective of the Bible.

Because Jesus is King, His words are now of utmost importance. In a republic, we vote on our laws, but in a kingdom, the words of the king are law. That makes a red-letter Bible extremely valuable. His words take on new significance.

The King is our source, and the rest of the New Testament is a commentary or unfolding of the basic truth that He gave us. The books of the Gospels—Matthew, Mark, Luke, and John—become the core of our Kingdom faith. Rereading Paul's letters with the Kingdom in mind now makes Paul so easy to understand, and we see how clearly he supports the Kingdom Gospel.

Colossians 1:13
Who hath delivered us from the power of darkness, and hath translated us into the kingdom of his dear Son.

Paul certainly expressed that we are in that kingdom now. He is saying the same things that the new believers were accused of claiming in the book of Acts. Peter's warnings about Paul's writings take on new meaning when we see some use his letters to place the

Kingdom far off in the future and ignore his clear statements on its present reality. Twisting scripture for the purpose of supporting a doctrine is rampant in the Christian world. If you are not on the kingdom topic, you are off target.

The Kingdom changes your perspective on Christian living.

As King, the words and decrees that Jesus issued become our standard laws. Just as we are law-abiding citizens in the United States, we need to be law-abiding citizens in the Kingdom.

Matthew 6:33 (GNT)
Be concerned above everything else with the
Kingdom of God and with what he requires
of you, and he will provide you with all these
other things.

The King James Version uses the word "righteousness," which implies being in right standing with the Kingdom's laws. Seek the Kingdom as a priority and be in alignment with its laws. From the Gospels, we can glean the laws we are to obey and carry out.

Parables are hidden truths. As King, Jesus's stories and parables are not fable or fairy tales. Most of the parables are truths about the Kingdom put in simple terms. They start with the phrase "The kingdom of

God is like . . ." That means listen up; here comes a truth you need to know about the Kingdom.

These parables give us extremely important information from the King as to the function and values of the Kingdom. One such parable gives us insight into how He will judge and determine your fate in eternity. In Matthew 25, the King talks about the end-time judgment when he will separate the sheep from the goats. He sends the goats into eternal punishment because of their deeds, not their beliefs. The judgment is based on behavior, not religious mental gymnastics. It's not a prayer they prayed or a confession they rendered. It's not a church they joined or a set of ritual obligations they performed. He judges them based on their deeds. Those deeds demonstrated whether they loved others. God expresses how He measures love: Love gives. Selfishness takes.

John 3:16
For God *so loved* the world, that *he gave* his
only begotten Son, that whosoever believeth
in him should not perish, but have
everlasting life.

His commandment to love one another is imperative. The world is full of takers, with far fewer givers who love others more than themselves. He describes the takers as those who gave no one food when they were hungry, or drink when they were thirsty, or clothes when they were naked, or time when they were lonely, or help when in need. What they believed set the direction of their life, but what they demonstrated in how they behaved mattered more. If Jesus is King, and He is, we need to heed His words and be careful not to follow the wayward teachings of those who do not understand the value of a benevolent King.

The Kingdom changes how we view Christianity.

Our culture teaches us to view Christianity as a religion. Jesus came and presented a government. When we view our relationship with Jesus through the lens of a government, we make our faith a daily experience. Being a citizen is a blessing far above the benefits of being a member. When you arrive in the Kingdom, you will view Christianity as a government, not a religion. It is a way of life. Seeing Jesus as King is the final step in elevating Him in your life to live on the throne of your heart. He is your King.

The Kingdom changes your perspective of salvation.

Ecclesiastes 12:13
Let us hear the conclusion of the whole matter: Fear God, and keep his commandments: for this is the whole duty of man.

Solomon summed the whole duty of man into a simple

verse with two tenants. The first is to fear God. It means to have respect for God. It means to hold Him in awe as the one with authority. Jesus said not to fear man, because all he can do is kill you. He said to fear the one who can not only kill you, but who has the authority to cast you into hell (Luke 12:4–5). We need a healthy reverence for the one eternal King who has authority over us.

The second part of King Solomon's insight is so important. It's what mankind and current religious trends tend to minimize. The rest of the duty of man is to obey that God, our King. Some current religions say it's all by grace. Others say it is all by election. Others deem it all by their correct doctrine or knowledge. But in every book of the Bible, by every author, there are two parts to salvation: first, whom do you fear, trust, or have faith in, and second, how do you act in accordance with that trust. These two are always connected. You can't escape the command to obey the King as part of your duty and requirement. Getting through the door of salvation is only the beginning. Being righteous, staying in tune with His commands, as Paul writes in Philippians 2:12, "work out your salvation with fear and trembling," is that second duty Solomon describes.

Ecclesiastes 12:14
For God shall bring every work into
judgment, with every secret thing, whether it
be good, or whether it be evil.

It seems insane that some religions teach, in our day, that grace, election, or something else gets them a free pass from having to obey the King and change the way that they live. Jesus, our King, said in John 14:15, "If you love me, keep my commandments."

King Jesus rules and reigns. Someday, He will move His throne to earth and rule and reign from here in a more forceful way. Now, we submit willingly. Then all will submit by the force of His word and authority. Some will yield willingly, some will submit while resisting, but all will bow before the King of Kings. Then you will understand how important the words of the King are. Happy are those who learn that lesson early.

Where is your allegiance? Are you an American first and a Christian second? Would you be at ease with Daniel in the lion's den because you know to which nation you adhere and which King has your back? As an immigrant going into the fiery furnace is a scary ordeal. But going through the fire as a *citizen* with heaven's state department behind you will give you confidence.

You have accepted Jesus as your savior and trust Him

to carry you into eternity. Now, trust Him to rule your daily life as your king. You have the opportunity to live the Kingdom life now.

APPENDIX A: JESUS IS A KING

Born a King

Matthew 2:1–2

There came wise men from the east to Jerusalem, saying, "Where is he that is born King of the Jews? for we have seen his star in the east, and are come to worship him." *(King by birthright)*

Introduced as a King

Matthew 3:1–2

In those days came John the Baptist, preaching in the wilderness of Judaea, saying, "Repent ye: for the kingdom of heaven is at hand."

(The King and His Domain are here now)

Acted Like a King

Matthew 7:29

For he taught them as *one* having authority, and not as the scribes.

(A King's words are law)

Presented to Jerusalem as a King

Zachariah 9:9 (ESV)

Rejoice greatly, O daughter of Zion; shout, O daughter of Jerusalem: behold, your King is coming to you: Righteous and having salvation is he, humble and mounted on a donkey, on a colt, the foal of a donkey.

Matthew 21:4–5

All this was done, that it might be fulfilled which was spoken by the prophet, saying, "tell the daughter of Jerusalem, Behold, thy King cometh, meek, and sitting upon a donkey, a colt, the foal of a donkey."

Charged with Claiming He Is a King

Matthew 27:11

Pilate, the governor asked him, "Are you the king of the Jews?" "Yes, I am," Jesus answered.

Declared King at His Death

Matthew 27:37

And set up over his head his accusation written, THIS IS JESUS THE KING OF THE JEWS.

Called King by His Followers

For the first three hundred years of Christianity, the "Way" was a kingdom, not a religion.

Acts 17:6–7

These that have turned the world upside down are come here also; and Jason has received them: and these all do contrary to Caesar, saying that there is another king, one Jesus. *(Followers referred to as citizens of the Kingdom, subjects of the King.)*

Colossians 1:13

Who hath delivered us from the power of darkness, and hath translated us into the kingdom of his dear Son.

Referred to as King by the New Testament

1 Timothy 1:17

Now unto the King eternal, immortal, invisible, the only wise God, be honor and glory for ever and ever. Amen.

Named King by the Old Testament Believers and the Angels

Revelation 15:3

And they sing the song of Moses the servant of God, and the song of the Lamb, saying, Great and marvelous are thy works, Lord God Almighty; just and true are thy ways, thou King of saints.

Titled King in Eternity

Revelation 19:16

And he hath on *his* vesture and on his thigh a name written, KING OF KINGS, AND LORD OF LORDS. *(Owner of owners.)*

(From eternity past to eternity future, there was never a day Jesus was NOT a King)

APPENDIX B: RESOURCES

Kingdom Resource Books

Rediscovering the Kingdom by Myles Munroe

The Principle and Power of Kingdom Citizenship by Myles Munroe

Kingdom Principles by Myles Munroe

The Unshakable Kingdom and the Unchanging Person by E. Stanley Jones

The Kingdom That Turned the World Upside Down by David W. Bercot

A Dictionary of Early Christian Beliefs, edited by David W Bercot

The Kingdom Field Guide by Brian C. Steele

The King and His Kingdom: Defining the Original Kingdom by Jason J. Allen

King, Kingdom, Citizen: His Reign and Our Identity by Tyler Dawn Rosenquist

The Ante-Nicene Fathers (10 Volume Set) by A. Cleveland Coxe, Alexander Roberts, James Donaldson

Nicen and Post-Nicene Fathers by Eusebius

Kingdom Internet Resources

Munroe Global, www.munroeglobal.com

Scroll Publishing by David Bercot,
www.scrollpublishing.com/david-bercot

Internet Archive,
www.archive.org/details/the-complete-ante-nicene-
nicene-and-post-nicene-church-fathers

The Real History of Constantine, by Simcha Jacobovici,
www.youtube.com/watch?v=_qYiwPBQ8Qg

Other Books by The Author

Forgive Instantly & Live Free

Being God: Stealing God's Power, Glory, and Kingdom

The Seeker's Guide to the Kingdom of God

ACKNOWLEDGMENTS

I thank my awesome wife, Patricia. She has made this incredible journey with me to the Promised Land. We left the world behind and trekked through the wilderness together to discover the Kingdom of God. The journey has been all the more pleasant having my best friend travel it with me. Thank you, Pat, for your patience, forbearance, steadfastness, and love for Jesus and me. My journey to the Kingdom would have been much harder without your companionship.

My deepest appreciation goes out to my consulting editors:

Mark Gulledge, Georgia

David Madden, Argentina

Sherry Schoendorf, Georgia

Vincent DeMasi, Pennsylvania

Tom Gurganus, North Carolina

My heart felt thankfulness is extended to the editing and publishing staff at BookLogix, Alpharetta, Georgia.

ABOUT THE AUTHOR

Terry Stueck is a graduate of Missouri State University and Faith Theological Seminary. He began inner-city mission work at the Bible Rescue Mission in the heart of Chicago's infamous Skid Row and the Pacific Garden Mission on Chicago's South Side. His missionary service extends to inner cities, church planting, church rescue, military installation communities, and prison ministry. In 1997, he founded High Plains Bible Mission in New Mexico as an outreach to native and inner-city communities. He currently serves as mission director.

Terry is also the author of *Forgive Instantly & Live Free*. It is the premier text and study guide for the "HOW TO" forgive the impossible. Its sequel, *Being God: Stealing God's Power, Glory, and Kingdom*, takes the reader to the next level as it explores God's ownership. *The Seeker's Guide to the Kingdom of God* gives the reader the key to living the kingdom life. We can know and acknowledge the King but are often blind to the parameters of His domain.

The Seeker's Guide
to the Kingdom of God

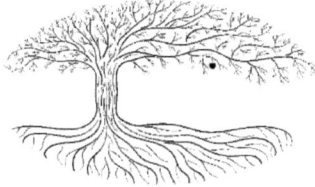

**A Kingdom consists two parts: a King and His domain.
Acknowledging Jesus as your King is monumental.
Comprehending His domain is critical.**

The Seeker's Guide to the Kingdom of God will give you the true domain perimeters that you need to stay in the favor of the King. The current Christian culture fails to educate the followers of Jesus in regard to the kingdom. Learn the boarders of His realm and live the Kingdom life now.

Entrance into the Kingdom of God Requires

- **A change in Citizenship**
- **A Change in Governments**
- **A Change in Allegiance**
- **A Change in Ownership**

Understanding the domain of God's Kingdom is essential. If you don't get this ownership principle correct, you will not be allowed into the Kingdom of God. Violating this principle will get you a ticket to the wilderness of Christian life.

**Available at www.forgiveinstantly.com, Amazon and
www.high-plains.org.**

www.ingramcontent.com/pod-product-compliance
Lightning Source LLC
Chambersburg PA
CBHW060443040426
42331CB00044B/2584